AF251849

Published by
Nutshell Brand Consultancy
604/163 Cremorne Street
Richmond, VIC 3121
Australia

www.nutshell.net.au



First published 2014
©Bryce Ott 2014
The moral right of the author has been asserted.
ISBN: 978-0-9923071-0-3 (Paperback)

Design by: ERD.COM.AU
Typeset by: Bearink

Printed in Australia by: Bambra Press

# CONTENTS

## PART ONE
## PRACTICAL THEORY



## PART TWO
## PUTTING THEORY INTO PRACTICE



### How to use this book

Brand Positioning in a Nutshell is designed to be used in conjunction
with a workbook where you develop your thinking as you read the book.
The workbook can be downloaded from the Nutshell website,
www.nutshell.net.au

# PART ONE
# PRACTICAL THEORY

This part of *Brand Positioning in a Nutshell* will quickly and efficiently get you up to speed with the concepts and terminology involved in unlocking the positioning of a brand.

# INTRODUCTION

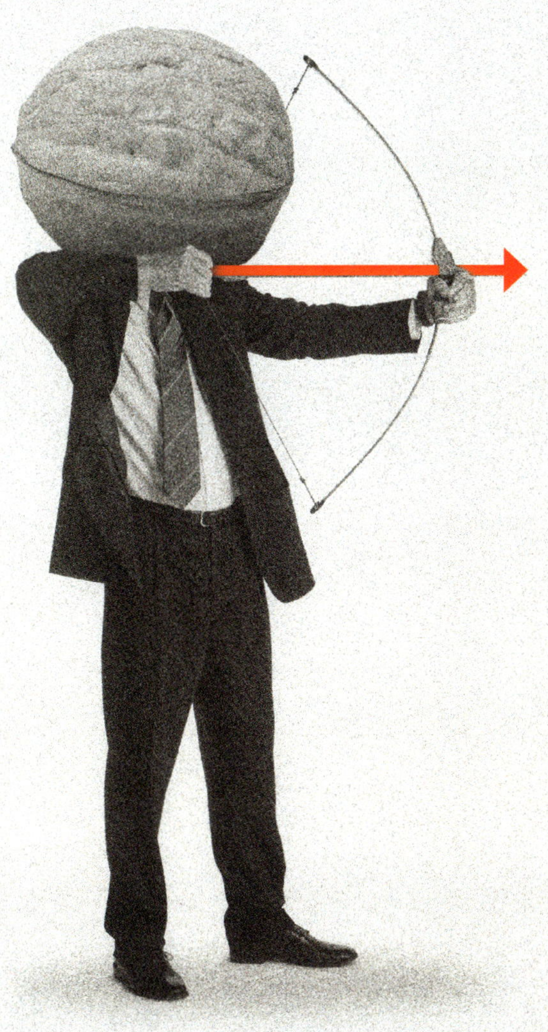

Would you like to be able to explain your business or product in a clear, compelling way **in 10 seconds or less**?

Would you like to be confident that you know exactly **who your organisation needs to talk to** and exactly **what it needs to say**?

Would you like **everyone** in your organisation to be **galvanised by the same vision** and aiming towards the same flag on the hill?

This book and its companion workbook will get you there.

*Brand Positioning in a Nutshell* is all about helping you unlock the ideal positioning of your brand. It takes a very practical, accessible approach that quickly covers theory and moves on to practice.

Chances are you've got a great story to tell, but can't find the right way to tell it.

I once worked with a family-owned manufacturing company that makes bathroom and kitchen fittings. The patriarch of the family was the founder of the business and an engineer. His natural tendency was to talk with great pride about the details of the machines he had designed or customised to achieve the precise tolerances required to make taps and fittings of a very high standard at a very affordable price point. The look of the end product was a bit of an afterthought for him. The beauty for him was in the technical excellence of his products. By the end of the brand positioning process I took them through, they were clear that what they really offered was 'meticulously designed tapware, without the designer prices'. The patriarch's daughter, who was in charge of marketing, said to me when I presented my recommendations, 'I'm so glad you see us as meticulous.' But they had always been meticulous. It was just a matter of identifying that as a defining trait of theirs and crafting the right words to capture the strength of their offer, from a technical as well as an aesthetic perspective.

*Brand Positioning in a Nutshell* is written for non-marketers, although it can help marketers as well. It guides you through a simple process I've successfully implemented for all kinds of brands in all sorts of categories, using clear, accessible, non-technical language.

If this happens to be the first book you read on the subject of brands, great! It's an excellent place to start, because it focuses strictly on brand positioning, which lays the foundation for everything else about brands. It doesn't mix brand strategy with business strategy, marketing strategy, logo design, brand management, or any other related but different disciplines. All these disciplines are connected, but I will help you tease them apart to ensure you're focused on brand positioning and understand its specific role relative to the others.

This is the only book I know of that focuses on starting with the basics and developing the right positioning to become the flag on the hill for your brand. As I see it, you can't do anything valuable with your brand until you have absolute clarity on what your brand positioning is. It's no secret why my business is called Nutshell Brand Consultancy!

I've met countless people working in many different organisations who all have variations on the same problem – they haven't found a clear, concise, compelling way to talk about what their brand has to offer. Sound familiar?

The solution is to strip back all the jargon and complexity to three clear, practical steps that do not require any marketing training or expertise. In this book, I:

1.  List and define the nine elements of a successful brand positioning.
2.  Provide simple questions and exercises to help you focus and define those nine elements as they apply to your brand.
3.  Guide you through a practical, logical system for evaluating the brand strategy you develop, to ensure it will work.

## REASONS YOU MIGHT BE READING THIS BOOK

Great literary scholars often say there are only seven basic stories in the world, so writing is about finding new and engaging ways for those stories to play out.

In 30 years of helping organisations work out the issues associated with their brands, I've found six stories that come up time and again. Who knows, maybe I'm missing one! Let's start with the six most common as a backdrop for talking about brand positioning. If literature is about finding new ways to flesh out classic stories, brand positioning is about finding specific ways to address classic challenges in defining a brand. See if you recognise yourself in any of these scenarios.

### 1) Too Busy Doing The Doing

As the Queen of Hearts famously said in *Alice in Wonderland* – 'My dear, here we must run as fast as we can, just to stay in place. And if you wish to go anywhere you must run twice as fast as that.'

What did you say last time someone asked how you are? You probably replied, 'Busy!' In fact, the person asking you probably said 'How are you? Busy?' It's almost a given in our culture that you're *supposed* to be busy. If you're not busy, you're falling behind.

But are you busy with things that are genuinely productive, things that are moving your organisation forward? Or are you spending three hours a day wading through hundreds of emails and five hours a day sitting in meetings, before you actually get to *do* anything?

I can't make emails and meetings go away, but I can promise that this book is a practical, efficient way to help you work *on* the business rather than *in* the business, so that doing the doing becomes more focused and more productive.

## 2) Herding Cats

It's a great image, isn't it? Cats are notoriously independent and free-thinking creatures. Trying to get them all marching neatly in the same direction is nearly impossible. This mental picture can be extremely relevant to any organisation that has more than two people in it as well.

Fortunately, people tend to respond a bit better to reasoning and relationship building than our feline friends. If you feel like you are spending your life herding cats, chances are you're dealing with an underlying *process* problem, more than a *content* problem. It may seem like the issue is finding the right answer, but it's more likely to be about reaching **consensus**. The process aspect of this book addresses this problem.

Consensus is literally half the battle. It's one of only two non-negotiable outcomes in developing a brand positioning that will be successfully implemented. The other one is **clarity**, but more about both of them later.

## 3) Nobody Understands Me

If you were a hormonal, angst-filled teenager moaning that no one understands you, we'd all make supportive noises whilst thinking to ourselves that it's just a matter of time before you grow out of this phase. But if you're part of an organisation trying to achieve its vision and goals, time isn't going to fix this. You need to.

If you struggle on a daily basis with agencies and other suppliers, or even staff who aren't giving you what you need because they don't understand what you're all about, then it's time to take responsibility for that yourself.

Ask yourself whether you're doing the best job you can in telling your brand story to people around you. Do they get it instantly and respond in a way that is productive and mutually beneficial? If the answer is no, don't panic, but do keep reading. We'll get you sorted out before you know it.

## 4) It's All About You

You're probably familiar with the visual metaphor of a swan that appears to glide effortlessly and gracefully across the water, while underneath the surface its feet are paddling furiously, unseen.

There's always going to be lots more going on with you than your customers need to, or want to, know about. Successfully positioning your brand requires that you step back from yourself and think about your offer from the perspective of your customer. Your customer wants the graceful swan, not the frantic paddling.

Another variation on making it all about you is something I call the 'If you build it, they will come' model, after the movie *Field of Dreams*. In the film, this approach worked out pretty well for Kevin Costner, but it doesn't turn out so well for many.

In this scenario, a business has a machine sitting around, so they figure out all the things it can make and then go see if anyone wants to buy them. Often it's done in the name of innovation, which is just a fancy name for change. There's no point in making changes unless they represent something somebody wants. Just ask the people responsible for Pepsi AM or Coke Zero.

Another version of this scenario is when someone makes something just because they know how to make it, or because it's what **they** like, without checking that it's something that people want. Sometimes it works, but it's the luck of the draw.

By following the steps in this book, you'll see how you can factor in your perspective without losing sight of your customer's perceptions, ensuring that you have a winning brand positioning.

## 5) Caught Up In The Detail

Detail is a funny thing. It strikes me as odd that both the expressions 'God is in the detail' and 'The devil is in the detail' are commonly used. Is attention to detail a good or a bad thing? Maybe it's both.

Pablo Picasso said 'One does a whole painting for one peach and people think just the opposite – that particular peach is but a detail.' Picasso was an amazing artist, but in my opinion he would not have made a good brand strategist.

The art of brand positioning is in seeing the big picture without losing sight of the details. Details may be how you manage your way to excellence, but the big picture is how you engage as a brand with customers, suppliers and colleagues.

A brand is what you stand for. An engineer at BMW could tell you all about the technical precision and quality of every part in one of their engines, but the BMW brand stands for The Ultimate Driving Machine. One is the detail. The other is the big picture. Seeing the difference between the two and learning how to capture and use them both is part of what you will learn in this book.

## 6) Your Light Is Under A Bushel

Surely this is the most basic problem of all. You're good at what you do, offer an excellent product or service and deliver on your promises. There just aren't enough people who know about what you have to offer.

In today's world, removing that bushel to let your light shine out is the role of marketing. Many businesses live or die based on their marketing prowess. In some organisations, it plays a smaller role. Maybe you're part of an organisation that just isn't marketing driven, so you can't justify having marketing professionals on staff. That doesn't mean it's not important to make sure that your target audience knows you're there and understands what you have to offer.

There's no doubt that marketing is going through a period of major change, driven largely by technology. Social media is redefining the marketing toolkit and people (marketers and non-marketers alike) are reinventing ways of getting the message of a brand out into the world.

That's why it's important to make a distinction between brand and marketing. Brand positioning underpins marketing strategy and needs to be identified first. Whether you're a blogger getting your story out via the internet, or a manufacturer making a niche product, the starting point is to go through a disciplined, structured process of defining your brand.

So, going back to the light under the bushel analogy, marketing is about removing the bushel and brand positioning is about describing the light in such a clear, compelling way that people can't wait to see it.

## 7) ?

Is there a scenario that describes the situation you face with your brand that I haven't described?

 This is a hands-on, DIY book, so let's start putting it into practice right now. Use your workbook (page 4) to jot down notes on the challenges you think are facing your organisation in relation to your brand. Feel free to identify multiple challenges from the list in this section, or describe others if none of the ones here quite capture your situation.

## OUTCOMES YOU CAN EXPECT FROM USING THIS BOOK

There are two words that are my mantra in developing a successful brand positioning:

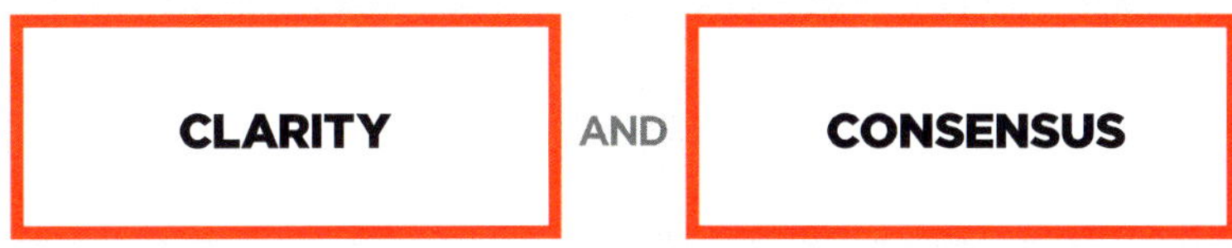


### Clarity

Clarity in a brand positioning is about articulating the vision for the brand in such a way that everyone who is exposed to the vision gets it instantly and understands it perfectly.

Having clarity means that everyone involved with the brand has a shared understanding of what is desired and expected from the brand. Having clarity means that everyone in the organisation can do their job independently, without the risk of making decisions in their particular area that will lead to the brand being presented inconsistently.

Achieving clarity is related to the content of the brand positioning. One key is to articulate the brand positioning concisely, using words that are telegraphic and not subject to diverse interpretations. You want to use as many words as you need to capture the core of what the brand has to offer, but as few words as possible to ensure that it is clear and streamlined.

Using the Nutshell model, we'll work through nine component parts of a brand positioning and bring it down to one key sentence, which will rarely be more than six or seven words. And the whole model will fit on one page.

### Consensus

Early on in my career, friends used to joke that one day I would have a consulting business and the tagline for that business would be, 'Shut up and do it my way!' Ouch!

Fortunately, I have acquired some decent listening skills since then and learned that it's difficult to get anywhere without engaging with people and working together to reach consensus.

Where clarity is about content, consensus is about process. The 'right' brand positioning can only be 'right' if it has buy-in from the various people in the organisation who will have a role in bringing the brand to life. And, realistically, that's pretty much everybody, isn't it? Don't worry, though, there are some good tips for designing a process that is more efficient than engaging with every single person in the organisation.

The bottom line is that you need to have **both** clarity and consensus for your brand positioning to be successful.

This simple chart summarises the importance of having both clarity and consensus.

| | |
|---|---|
| **Clarity without Consensus** | If everyone understands the brand positioning, but they don't believe in it, they will find opportunities to do a 'better' job and the brand will appear inconsistent or schizophrenic. |
| **Consensus without Clarity** | If everyone thinks they agree with the brand positioning but they are interpreting it differently, the execution will be inconsistent despite their best intentions and the brand will appear inconsistent or schizophrenic. |
| **Both Clarity and Consensus** | Only when all key stakeholders have a shared understanding and commitment to the brand positioning, will it be executed consistently and well. |

My favourite thing about what I do for a living is the 'Aha' moment. It happens when a client sees everything that's been spinning around in their head come together and settle into a clear, concise summary that captures their brand in a powerful way. I see the fog lift and a light go on in their eyes telling me they know their brand positioning is going to galvanise their organisation and drive their business forward. Everyone on the team says 'That's it! That's us!' often in disbelief that they didn't think of it themselves.

They have achieved clarity and consensus.

This book packs my 30 years of experience into a practical guide to achieving that 'Aha' moment for your brand. Reading it and applying it is like hiring a consultant for the price of a book.

Before we get into the main content of this book, let me tell a brief story about a failure that has haunted me for most of my adult life. Perhaps this is a controversial way to start a book designed to motivate you and fill you with confidence, but it partly explains why this book exists and the reason that what it sets out to help you achieve is so important to me.

In my late teens, I read a book called *Stranger in a Strange Land*, by Robert Heinlein. He's a wonderful science fiction writer and it's a great book.

In it, the central character is an alien who comes to earth with no understanding of the way humans think, feel and behave. The extraordinary thing about this character, and one of the key premises of the book, is that he has an ability to grasp what is going on with people around him that far exceeds human notions of 'understanding' or 'empathy'. In fact, Heinlein had to invent a word to capture the concept. That word is 'grok'. It's a verb. 'To grok' means something like 'to understand so completely as to become one with'.

I was so taken by this brilliant concept that I took it upon myself to try to get this word into common usage. I would drop it casually into conversations and then provide an enthusiastic explanation of the meaning in response to the blank faces staring at me. What seemed self-evident in its value to me just didn't connect with my friends. I failed miserably in my campaign to gain common acceptance of the word 'grok'. Maybe it just sounds too funny. Or maybe it was just way ahead of its time.

In any case, I went on to become a brand strategist on a mission to help organisations find the story of their brand and articulate it so well that all their stakeholders, prospects and customers understand their brand so completely as to become one with it.

So, if you're ready to get clear on the story for your brand to take it to the next level, let's get started!

**CHAPTER 2**

# BRAND POSITIONING IN CONTEXT

## OVERVIEW AND DEFINITIONS

### Brand

Before I begin to discuss any aspects of brand positioning or brand strategy, it is important that I define what I mean when I use the word 'brand'. For purposes of this book, when I refer to brand, I mean:

**The complete set of perceptions, attitudes and experiences that an individual has with a product, service, or organisation.**

The first thing to notice in that definition is that it refers to an individual. The implication of referring to an individual is that a **brand is what your target audience thinks it is**, not necessarily what you think it is. It's a case of 'perception is reality'. Your job is to establish a set of desired perceptions of the brand, and then to develop strategies for shifting perceptions to align with that vision.

The second thing to keep in mind is that it's about perceptions, attitudes and experiences. This starts with the rational attributes of a product, but goes much further. How the brand makes them feel, what the brand says about them to others, the personality of the brand, how they interact with it, what they hear and see about it from other people, anyone who represents the brand in front of customers, are all part of the brand. Much of this is not tangible and rational. Emotions play a huge role in forging a connection between people and brands.

Now let's look at where Brand Positioning fits in the context of managing a business.

## Business Strategy

I use the term 'business' for the sake of simplicity, but by it I mean any organisation offering a product or a service.

It's important to make a distinction between your brand and your business.

They are closely related, but business strategy has to come first.

Business strategy is the discipline of working out how to maximise the long-term value of a business and how it will need to be structured and run in order to succeed. Business strategy is more fundamental, more nuts and bolts than brand strategy. It focuses on areas including:

- Goals and Objectives
- Market size
- Existence and size of niches
- Availability of 'white space' that represents untapped opportunities
- Competitor strengths and weaknesses
- Costs of entry
- Ability to achieve and sustain differentiation/competitive advantage
- Operational requirements
- Sourcing of materials, talent, information, etc

## Brand Positioning

Brand positioning is the discipline of defining **what** you do, **how** you do it, **why** you do it and **who** you do it for, in a way that is **clear** and **compelling**.

For some reason, I've been noticing a lot of ads for mascara lately. It seems like there's been an explosion of new product development in that category. The ads talk about attributes like various types of brushes and interesting ingredients like collagen. They talk about curling, lifting, extending, adding volume, defining, lasting and waterproofing. But those attributes and functions are merely a means to an end. Ultimately, they are aiming to make an emotional connection with women, promising to help them get attention, make an impression, be noticed.

Brand positioning is about structuring the overall story that will make the brand appealing.

## Brand Strategy

This term is probably the most confusing, because it is used so inconsistently. For some, it is interchangeable with brand positioning.

In graphic design companies, it is often used to describe the brief for logo development. With the emergence of digital and social media, many people use the term when they are actually talking about how the brand will use a particular medium or how the brand will be represented via its website.

I will use the term brand strategy to refer to the discipline of bringing the brand positioning to life across all aspects of how the brand manifests itself, from product to logo to customer service to marketing, etc.

## Logo

I include this term in this section only because people so often use the word brand when they're talking about the logo. A brand is much more than a logo, which is the symbol, or mark, that brands use to represent themselves visually.

A logo is a sort of signature. Obviously, you are much more than your signature. The same is true of a brand. The brand positioning should come first and be reflected in the logo. As brands evolve, sometimes their logo needs to evolve as well.

## Marketing and Marketing Strategy

Marketing strategy should come after the business strategy and brand strategy have been developed.

Many people would consider brand strategy to be a part of marketing strategy, but let me explain why I make a distinction.

Getting the story of your brand out there needs to happen in two steps:

- Define what that story is
- Find the most effective and efficient ways to get that story out there

If you don't do things in that order, you risk wasting money on telling the wrong story and/or telling it to the wrong people.

Defining the right story for your brand is what I'm talking about when I refer to brand positioning. Getting that story out to your target audiences is what I'm talking about when I refer to marketing.

Marketing strategy is traditionally described as the discipline of managing the four P's:

- Product
- Price
- Place (distribution)
- Promotion

By optimising each of the four P's and how they work together, you maximise the results that come from marketing – brand awareness, consideration, trial, loyalty and advocacy. And importantly, you maximise sales and profitability.

## Marketing Activity

Once you've got your marketing strategies in place, you move on to the actual marketing, which is the tactical campaigns and programs that get the story of your brand out there. They need to be grounded in good marketing strategy, which needs to be grounded in a good brand strategy.

## Business vs. Brand – A discussion on why both have to be right

It is possible to have an excellent business strategy without giving any thought at all to brand positioning. Many organisations focus on doing the doing and hope for the best when it comes to creating perceptions of their brand and attracting customers. When you're exceptionally good at what you do, you can even get away with it, relying on word of mouth to build your reputation. In that scenario, you'll always be left wondering how much further you could have gone if you'd taken an active role in managing your brand, based on carefully developing your brand positioning.

It's also possible to have a good brand without having a good business, though that scenario tends to be short-lived. Kodak had a great brand, but when they miscalculated the future of photography and rejected all things digital, they got left behind and the business fell apart. No amount of brand resonance can ultimately compensate for a poor business.

A strong business has:

- Good product
- Good management of staff, risk, operations, etc
- Good processes
- Good supplier and partner relationships
- Good business model

A strong brand has:

- Good awareness
- Clear, powerful positioning
- Positive, accurate perceptions
- Good conversion from awareness, to consideration, to trial, to loyalty, to advocacy

The following diagram represents the four possible scenarios resulting from combinations of a strong or weak business and strong or weak brand.

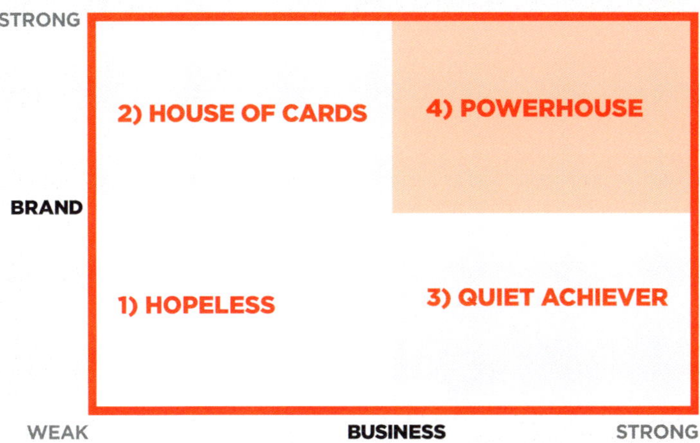


1. The combination of weak business and weak brand is **hopeless** and doomed to fail. In fact, it is unlikely to get off the ground in the first place without losing lots of money. It certainly won't get any traction in the marketplace.

2. The combination of a strong brand and a weak business is a **house of cards** that will collapse at the first stress. Kodak is a good example of a situation where the business had once been very good, but lost relevance. The strength of the brand was not enough to sustain it. Borders Bookstores is another example. From a brand perspective, it was very appealing to a large number of people. The idea of combining a bookstore with a café was popular and differentiating from other bookstores. The problem was that the business model wasn't strong enough to hold up in a market where bookstores were struggling to survive. People liked Borders, but the business apparently didn't make enough money to survive. Borrowed interest can also fuel brand appeal, but it doesn't guarantee a good business. Celebrity-driven brands are common examples:

In 2008, Natalie Portman created a line of vegan-friendly footwear in a partnership with a New York City store. The shoes, which retailed for $200 a pair, were created without fur, leather or feathers. Natalie is a talented actress and her personal brand no doubt generated interest in her footwear range, but the business model didn't stack up and the range was discontinued within a year.

The Kardashian sisters, Kim, Khloe and Kourtney are certainly a brand with well-established appeal, especially among young people. Their brand, however, was not strong enough to drive the success of their own credit card called the Kardashian Kard, aimed at young adults and backed by MasterCard. The card carried high fees and was cancelled almost immediately after it launched.

3. The combination of strong business and weak brand can work, but is unlikely to reach its full potential, remaining a **quiet achiever**. By definition, you'll struggle to find high-profile examples for this category, because they have weak brands. But they do exist. One example might be a great restaurant that's been there forever, but outside a small number of loyal diners, nobody knows about it. Or an IT-support company that does a great job and gets lots of repeat business and word of mouth referrals, but has no idea how to sell itself.

There are also many examples among not-for-profit organisations. They tend to be passionate about what they do and make a fantastic contribution to the community or the world, but don't engage in any sort of brand-building activities because they think it's somehow inappropriate to spend money on marketing, or they can't tear themselves away from doing the doing to talk about it. Even when they take on board the value of marketing themselves and getting their story out, they are often so passionate and caught up in the details of what they do and how important it is, that they struggle to clearly and concisely explain their offer to outsiders.

Several years ago, I did some brand strategy work for a not-for-profit run by a private foundation. Their mission is to contribute to the development of what they call 'The Good Society'. From the start, I never really understood that phrase and knew that it wasn't helping them. They wanted to help create a society with values and integrity, one that was civilised and morally strong. Referring to some abstract concept called 'The Good Society' sounded very old-fashioned, stuffy and patrician, at least to my ear. It's a good example of something that has currency and relevance within an organisation, but just doesn't translate well when the brand tries to communicate with outsiders.

The core product of the foundation is a colloquium (another old-fashioned, stuffy term), which brings together nominated individuals from three key sectors of society – the public sector (government and policy-makers), the private sector (mostly business people), and the not-for-profit sector (social services, the arts, etc.). Each colloquium brings together 20 or so people who are seen to be future leaders from across those three sectors. The group spends a week discussing a series of readings from important philosophical writers across history and exploring the moral and ethical questions for society that the readings bring up.

They had a good 'business', always receiving great reviews from participants as well as management in the organisations who'd nominated the participants, but the brand was letting them down. Because the brand wasn't clear or strong, they had to spend a disproportionate amount of time selling their programme through personal contacts and driving it through word of mouth. To the private sector, it all seemed a bit abstract and esoteric, which meant they found it particularly difficult to recruit the number of private sector participants they needed to keep the groups balanced. What I did for them was explore their story and try to bring some clarity to it, so that their target audiences would understand it instantly and see it's relevance.

The one-line summary that I wrote for them was 'Cultivating Wisdom in Leadership'. 'Leadership' is much easier for organisations to understand than 'The Good Society', so it was much more relevant to the target audience and much easier to recommend as part of a training budget, which is how participation in the colloquium would normally be funded.

Nothing else changed fundamentally about the organisation or the programme, but the shift from 'Pursuing The Good Society' to 'Cultivating Wisdom In Leadership' formed the basis for them to grow to the point where they are running many more sessions of the colloquium each year and have a waiting list of participants, even in the private sector.

When you look at the four scenarios in the chart above, it becomes clear that outcomes for any organisation or brand are really only maximised when both the business and the brand are strong.

4.  The combination of a strong business and a strong brand is the powerhouse we all aim for. Being in this quadrant means that your business offers something that customers genuinely want, you deliver it well and the complete set of perceptions and experiences of the customer are clear and positive.

## Summary

This book is not designed to help you design a strong business, but I urge you to evaluate the strength of your business before you focus on defining and building your brand. This book is about leveraging a strong business into a strong brand and maximise the success of the business.

This is also not specifically a book about marketing or marketing strategy, but if you master the principles of this book and apply them to your brand, you will have the flag on the hill for your marketing strategy and marketing programmes, to make sure that every dollar you spend on marketing is taking the business in the right direction.

Now we have clear definitions of the various aspects of strategy that relate to your business and a clear definition of what brand positioning is and how it figures in the mix.

The rest of the book is about actually finding the right story for your brand, so that it works as hard as possible for you.

**CHAPTER 3**

# DEFINING WHAT 'RIGHT' MEANS FOR YOUR BRAND

This book is designed to help you find the right story for your brand, the right brand positioning. Before we go into the process of developing your brand positioning, it's worth taking some time to explore how you'll know when you've found the right answers.

Brand positioning isn't like mathematics. There are many ways to be right. It's a subjective area. While there aren't really any rigid formulas that guarantee success, there are principles that work well in driving a rigorous process of finding the right answer for your brand.

In order to take as much of the subjectivity as possible out of the process, you can lock in some criteria for evaluating the strategies you come up with.

## SETTING THE CONTEXT – A PROCESS FOR MANAGING YOUR BRAND

Let's look at the big picture of brand management as a process, because it will help you get clarity on what you're hoping to achieve with your brand positioning.

The brand management process is often depicted as a circle, as in the following diagram.

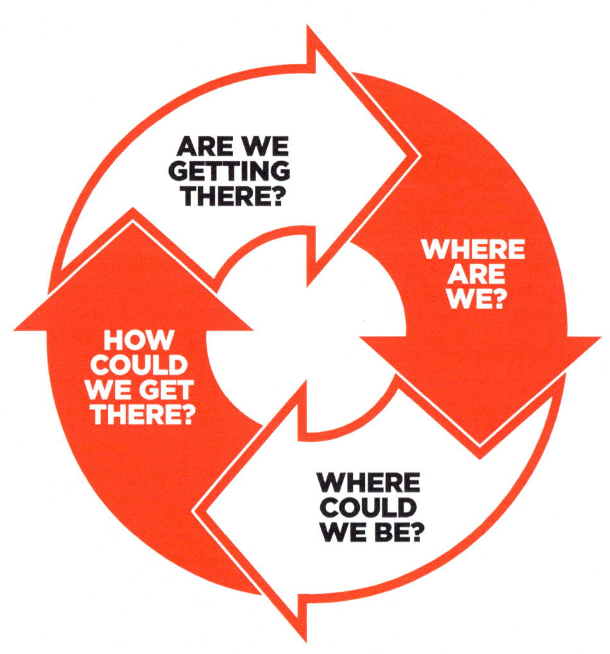

The diagram is in the shape of a circle because the process of brand management is continuous. Whether you plan and manage your business and your brand in cycles of a week, a month or a year, the end of each cycle is the beginning of the next one.

**Where are we now** is a summary of the current status of the business in terms of key factors that capture the big picture of the brand. This should include:

Q  Category definition – what's the competitive frame of reference where customers are considering the brand?

Q  Product – what products or services is the brand offering in that category?

Q  Customer – who does the brand sell to?

Q  Distribution – what channels is the brand selling through?

Q  Performance – sales volume, market share, distribution levels and any other key performance indicators

**Where could we be** works with those same key factors, but invites you to cast your mind forward to the medium and long-term future of the brand and imagine what the parameters of the brand will be then.

Q  Are there other products or services that you would like to launch?

Q  If you expanded your offer with new products or services, would that change the competitive frame, or category definition, where you operate?

Q  Could you grow just by selling your existing products or services to new customers or customer segments?

Q  Could you grow just by selling your existing products or services to the same type of customers, but through additional channels (eg by selling via the internet, or moving from pharmacies only to pharmacies plus supermarkets)?

**How could we get there** is the more pragmatic stage, where you work through what you would have to do in order to get from where you are now to where you could be.

Q  To add additional products or services, would you need a new factory or production line, new overseas contacts for importing goods, new staff with required technical skills?

Q  To reach new customers, would you need research into market segments, additional marketing resources, new product variants?

Q  To gain additional distribution, would you need more or different sales staff, new shipping or storage capabilities, new product formulations to achieve longer shelf life?

**Are we getting there** is about measurement. As the saying goes, you can only manage what you measure. Whatever the cycle you are planning for, you need to be able to measure the progress you make from 'where we are now' to 'where we could be' in order assess your success.

At the end of each planning cycle, you have a new 'where are we now', which becomes the basis for a new 'where could we be' and the process begins again.

Clearly, then, it is important to define your business objectives before you start work on your brand positioning.

If you haven't already thought this through, there are some simple guidelines to help you set the business context for your brand strategy in Chapter 7.

## THREE FILTERS FOR 'RIGHT' – THE BRAND POSITIONING TRIFECTA

There are three filters that you should put your thinking through before you're confident that you have the right story for your brand. I call these three filters the 3 D's and frame them up as three simple questions you should ask about the positioning you come up with:

### Deliverable

Q  Can the business genuinely provide what you are promising with the brand?

### Desired

Q  Is the story of your brand relevant and compelling to the customer you have in mind?

### Differentiating

Q  Is the story of your brand different enough from your competitors to motivate your target audience to choose your brand over theirs?

What you're looking for is a brand positioning that occupies the sweet spot in the diagram opposite, where you deliver on all three criteria. A brand positioning that is deliverable, desired and differentiating gives you the best chance of making your brand successful.

If you draft a brand positioning that can't answer yes to one or more of the three questions, there will be a risk to the success of the brand. Having said that, there will also be some general implications about what you can do to turn a 'no' into a 'yes'.

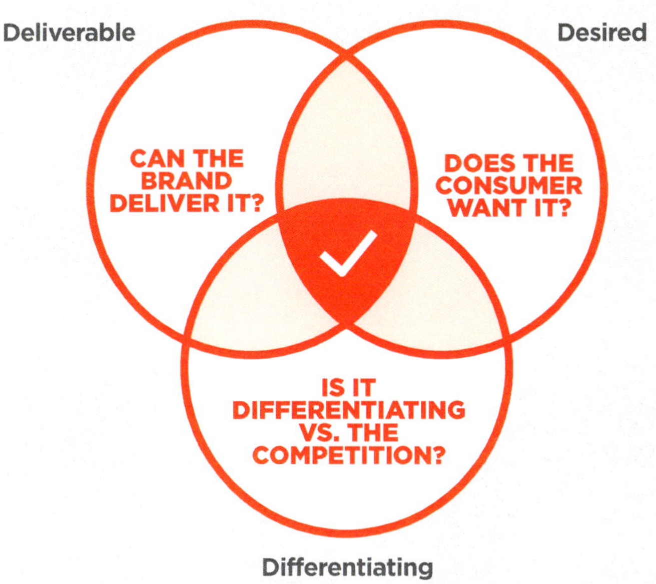


There are three possible scenarios to consider, where your business has only two of the three criteria nailed:

Your brand positioning is compelling to the target audience and differentiating from the competition, but there are doubts about whether the business can deliver on it.

This scenario is most likely to come up when you have an idea first and are trying to build a business around it. Or perhaps you have an existing business that you're trying to expand or evolve to capture a proven opportunity, but haven't yet worked out the operational side of turning the opportunity into a reality.

If you find yourself in this situation, don't give up, but you need to go back to your business strategy and resolve the business issues holding you back before the right brand positioning can be successfully implemented in the marketplace.

Remember, telling a compelling brand story to interested customers and failing to deliver on it with your product or service will only alienate those customers, generate negative word of mouth, and damage your business.

This book can help you develop the right story for the brand you want to build, but it won't replace getting back to basics and getting the business strategy right.

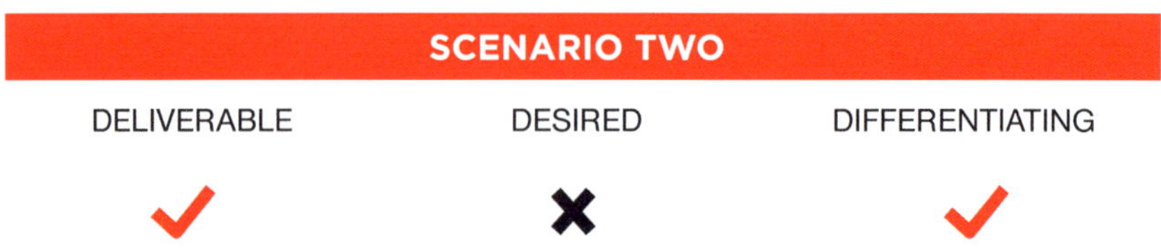


The business can deliver and the offer is differentiating from the competition, but it's not something the target audience wants or it's not positioned in a way that is appealing to the target audience.

At first glance, this sounds like a disaster waiting to happen. You've got the ability to make a product that is differentiated from your key competitors, which is great, but if no one wants to buy it, that's irrelevant.

If you follow the logic of the Nutshell process, you probably wouldn't find yourself in this scenario, because the Nutshell process advocates that you start by defining your target audience and summarising how they think, feel and behave in your category. If you do that, you will be unlikely to find yourself with a product they don't want, because you would have developed a product based on an understanding of what they do want.

But there may be a way to turn the situation around and make lemonade out of what appears to be lemons at the moment.

Take the story of Post-it notes as an example.

The 3M Company was founded in the US in 1902 by five businessmen. It was originally called the Minnesota Mining and Manufacturing Company and has a long history of creativity and innovation in new product development. The most famous of those stories is undoubtedly the one about Post-it notes. It's a great example of setting out to develop one thing, but ending up with something altogether different that turns into a huge opportunity.

One of 3M's chemists, Dr Spencer Silver, was working on a super-strong adhesive in 1968. In the course of his work, one of his 'failed' attempts was in fact just the opposite of what he set out to create. It was a very weak adhesive, which stuck gently and didn't hold things together permanently or with any great strength.

The adhesive did not meet the specifications he had been given. Based on the target audience he was focused on and the insight that the target audience was looking for something that would stick things together very strongly, that particular attempt failed. But Dr Spencer felt the substance had potential for other applications, though he never managed to convince his employer what they might be or that the product was worth pursuing.

Five years later, Art Fry – a colleague of Dr Silver's – famously remembered Silver's adhesive product when he was struggling with bookmarks that kept falling out of his hymnal at church. He came up with the idea of using the adhesive on bits of paper to attach them as bookmarks to the pages in his hymnal without damaging the book. It was another five years before 3M began distributing the product nationally.

Dr Silver created a product that 3M could definitely make and that was clearly differentiated from anything else on the market, but it was Art Fry who found the consumer insight that turned it into something that was appealing to people. Between the two of them, they found a brand story that hit the sweet spot in the positioning trifecta.

It is definitely a good idea to always ground yourself in the consumer's perspective, but don't be afraid to be creative either. If you genuinely understand your target audience and have real insight into what's important to them, you may very well find a new and innovative solution that combines what you can deliver and what people want, as well as being differentiating from the competition.

<table>
<tr><th colspan="3" style="background-color:#F15A22;color:white">SCENARIO THREE</th></tr>
<tr><td>DELIVERABLE</td><td>DESIRED</td><td>DIFFERENTIATING</td></tr>
<tr><td>✔</td><td>✔</td><td>✘</td></tr>
</table>

The business can deliver on the brand positioning and your story is compelling to the target audience, but it's not differentiating from the competition.

I always think of the classic local pizza shop when I think of this scenario. How many pizza boxes have you seen that say 'You've tried the rest. Now try the best!' Of course it's impossible for them all to be the best. In fact, the reality is pretty much the opposite – they're all more or less the same.

So the only differentiation is based on convenience – you pick the place closest to home. It's okay for geographic proximity and convenience to be your point of differentiation, but it's a bit risky because all it takes is for another business to make themselves available to your target audience and suddenly you're vulnerable.

The biggest trap in assessing whether your brand is effectively differentiated is not being honest with yourself about how your brand is performing. Many organisations have a culture where it's subtly discouraged to be at all critical of the brand or the business. You're seen as not being a team player if you say anything negative or you identify any weakness in the brand.

It's important to avoid that trap and objectively identify any weaknesses, in order to fix them. The customer certainly isn't going to buy your brand just because you insist on telling yourself you're the best.

If in doubt, it's best to get feedback from the customer. They will be much more objective about whether your product is differentiated and, after all, it's their perception that matters most in terms of what brand they choose to buy. We'll talk more about how to get consumer feedback in Chapter 8.

## More About Differentiation

Of the three filters in the brand positioning trifecta, my core belief is that Deliverability and Desirability are the two most important to focus on when developing the story of what you want to offer the marketplace through your brand.

The people I admire and the businesses I most enjoy working with, are the ones where there is a strong commitment to delivering something of value. To be of genuine value, the brand's offer has to be something that the customer genuinely wants (desirable) and the business has to be passionate about delivering it, well and consistently (deliverable).

Be true to what you have to offer and to your chosen customer, then you can worry about tweaking your offer to make it even better than your competitors.

The truth is that differentiation isn't as difficult to achieve as you might think. A brand can be differentiated on virtually any of the elements of a brand strategy.

Here are a few examples just to give you an idea:

- Differentiation based on target audience

| INSURANCE | |
| --- | --- |
| Brand One | Targets retirees and pensioners |
| Brand Two | Targets young singles just starting out |

| ANTIPERSPIRANTS | |
| --- | --- |
| Brand One | Targets women |
| Brand Two | Targets men |

- Differentiation based on attributes

| FRUIT JUICE | |
| --- | --- |
| Brand One | No artificial ingredients or preservatives |
| Brand Two | 80% real fruit juice |

| VACUUM CLEANER | |
| --- | --- |
| Brand One | Bag-less technology |
| Brand Two | Made in Germany |

- Differentiation based on functional benefit

| TOOTHPASTE | |
| --- | --- |
| Brand One | Removes tartar |
| Brand Two | Whitens teeth |

| MOISTURISER | |
| --- | --- |
| Brand One | Protects dry skin longer |
| Brand Two | Won't irritate sensitive skin |

- Differentiation based on emotional end benefit

## CARS

| | |
|---|---|
| Brand One | Makes you feel safe |
| Brand Two | Makes you feel adventurous |

## COMPUTERS

| | |
|---|---|
| Brand One | Makes you feel leading-edge and stylish |
| Brand Two | Makes you feel competent and conservative |

- Differentiation based on brand personality

## WATCHES

| | |
|---|---|
| Brand One | Sporty and outdoorsy |
| Brand Two | Elegant and sophisticated |

## BEER

| | |
|---|---|
| Brand One | Working class |
| Brand Two | Worldly |

- Differentiation based on values and drivers

## SHAMPOOS

| | |
|---|---|
| Brand One | About being environmentally responsible |
| Brand Two | About being clinically effective |

## FASHION LABELS

| | |
|---|---|
| Brand One | About the latest trends and fashionability |
| Brand Two | About comfort and wearability |

Too often, organisations feel compelled to keep developing new variations on a theme, for the sake of differentiation and innovation. This often leads to products that are different, but not better.

Milk is a great example of a category trying desperately to create differentiation. There's a lovely ad where a man comes into a milk bar and asks for a carton of milk. Exhausted, the woman behind the counter asks him if he wants 'Low fat, no fat, full cream, high calcium, high protein, soy, light, skim, omega 3, high calcium with vitamin D and folate, or extra dollop?' He looks completely overwhelmed and says, 'I just want milk that tastes like real milk.'

Since that ad came out, there's now a new ad telling us about something called permeates (whatever they are!). The brand being advertised is trying to differentiate itself by assuring us that it doesn't contain this mysterious, unknown and presumably undesirable ingredient.

Unless your differentiation also meets the desirability requirement in the brand strategy trifecta, there's a good chance you'll just end up confusing the consumer and fragmenting the category rather than building it.

Marketers and advertisers love to talk about a product's point of difference. The problem is that they tend to feel most comfortable if that point of difference is rational and functional. That's how we end up with a retailer offering 'buy now and pay nothing for six months', which a competitor responds to with 'buy now and pay nothing for 12-months', which leads to a head-to-head battle that escalates to 18-months, 24-months, etc. I've even seen examples offering up to 48-months interest free. By the time you pay for the item, you'll be shopping for its replacement, because it will have worn out!

Brands that stand for something on a deeper, less rational level, are less likely to need to resort to price cutting and sales tactics, because they are differentiated in ways that lead to customer loyalty. The classic example these days is Apple, but there's also Mercedes, Rolex, Mont Blanc, BOSE and many others.

It is not only high-end luxury brands that manage to achieve this meaningful level of differentiation. Coke and MacDonalds are much more about brand personality and imagery than anything rational.

Banks spend millions of dollars trying to change people's perceptions of their values and personality, not changing the details of their products and their interest rates.

So, as we get into the chapter on writing your brand positioning, where you put all the pieces of the puzzle together for your brand, just focus on what your brand does best and the core customer you have in mind when thinking about what the brand has to offer. We'll worry about differentiation after that.

**CHAPTER 4**

# ELEMENTS OF A BRAND POSITIONING

This chapter provides a detailed discussion of the nine elements that make up a sound brand positioning:

- Category Definition
- Target Audience Definition
- Target Audience Insights
- Brand Attributes
- Functional Benefits
- End Benefits
- Brand Personality
- Brand Values/Drivers
- Core Promise

You will need to work through these key elements to create the outline of the conversation you want to have to get your brand understood, so you can tell the right story to the right people.

The main purpose of this chapter is to introduce the terminology and explain the different elements of a brand positioning. This will form the foundation for actually writing your own brand positioning, which I'll guide you through in Chapter 11.

Organisations develop brand strategies to articulate their positioning in the market. I think of it as planting a flag on the hill, demonstrating how they want their brand to be perceived. Once the flag on the hill exists, everyone involved with the brand can take part, acting in a coordinated effort, marching step by step towards that flag. When the process is undertaken correctly, the organisation achieves clarity and consensus around how they want their brand to be perceived by their target audiences.

If the terminology and language in the above list is unfamiliar to you or sounds very corporate and academic, be patient — it will soon make sense.

Occasionally, when I consult for not-for-profit organisations or those involved in the caring fields such as social services, aged care, faith-based groups, etc., I find there is some discomfort in using marketing language and commercial concepts.

If you or some of the stakeholders in your organisation fall into that category, think of the brand positioning as the story of your organisation. Not 'story' as in its history and chronology, though that can be part of it, but rather 'story' in the sense of the essence of what you're all about, the core things that someone would be interested in learning about you to get to know your brand and connect with it. People buy brands they like, which results from much more than the rational aspects of what ingredients are in your product, how big your factory is or how long you've been around.

By working through all nine elements of a brand positioning, you will work out the full story for your brand that will help make it successful.

This is the model I use for summarising a brand positioning:

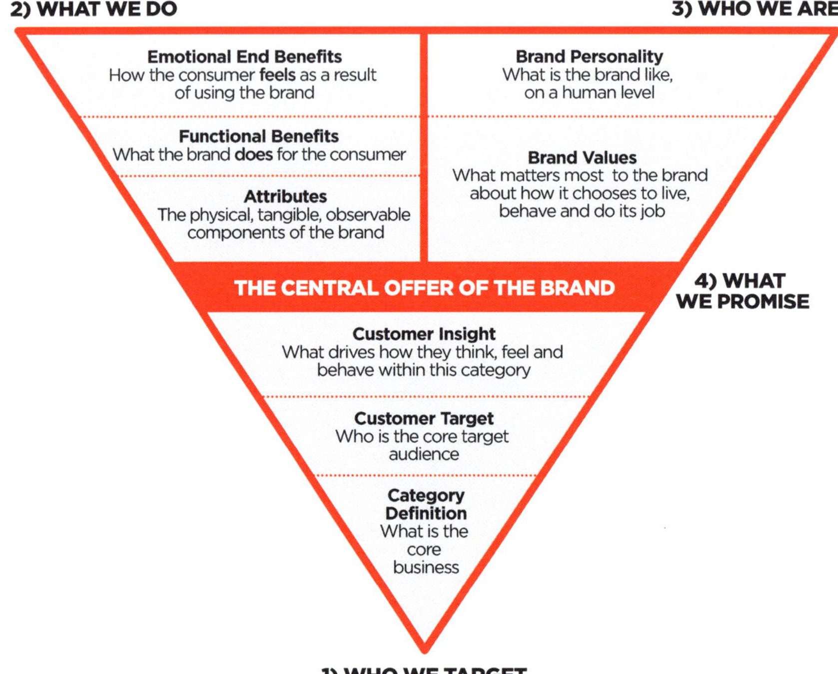

It divides up the nine elements into four groups:

1. Who we target
2. What we do
3. Who we are
4. What we promise

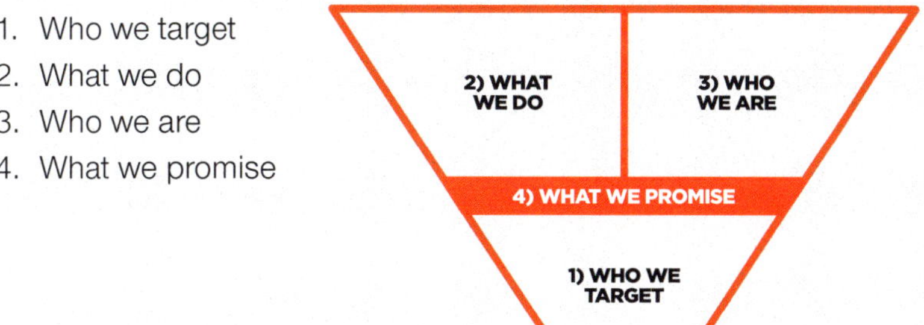


As you'll discover, it's important to work through the four groupings contained in the model in that order.

## Group 1 – Who Are You Targeting?

If you think of brand positioning as the clear outline of the conversation you need to have in order to get your brand understood, it makes sense that you need to know who you're having that conversation with first and foremost.

You can't have a real conversation unless you know something about the person you're talking to and are both interested in the topic you're talking about. Otherwise, it becomes a series of monologues where people are talking at one another rather than with one another, which is unlikely to be engaging or lead to any real connection. This becomes obvious when you think of it as a conversation, but it's amazing how often I need to remind clients that you need to start with the category definition and target audience.

So, the starting point of the conversation, or the development of your story, is **who am I talking to** and **what are we talking about**?

The Nutshell model for summarising a brand strategy is a triangle balancing on one of its three points. This first part of the story is graphically depicted as the point of the triangle on which the whole thing balances. I show it this way to remind myself and my clients that if you don't get this first group right, the whole thing will topple over and come crashing down.

There are three elements of the brand positioning that fit within this first part of the model:

- Category Definition
- Target Audience(s)
- Target Audience Insights

## Category Definition

Being clear about your category definition helps define what your conversation, or story, is about. It defines the context of the conversation you hope to have.

Think of it as answering the question, 'What business are you in?'

By answering this question, you take a stand on who you will be competing with, which forms the basis for assessing whether your brand positioning will be successful in convincing your target audience to choose your brand over your competitors.

## Target Audience

It's important to get clear on your target audience at the beginning of the process of writing your brand strategy because it's really hard to have a conversation if you don't know who you're talking to.

The trap that many organisations fall into, because they look inward rather than outward, is defining their target audience essentially as 'people who want what I'm selling.' While it may be true that the target audience for nail polish is women who paint their nails, it's not a terribly useful way to start the conversation or help you decide what the right story for your brand might be. It only identifies the person as someone shopping your category. It's a start, but it's hardly enough.

Defining your target audience doesn't need to go particularly deep, but it needs to cover the basics. Think of the target audience as the screening criteria for identifying the person you want to talk to.

Basics include:

- Gender
- Age
- Income
- Occupation
- Employment Status
- Education
- Ethnic or Cultural Background
- Life Stage
- Geography
- Core vs. Secondary Target Audience

## Target Audience Insights

Having outlined a description of your target audience, the next step is to summarise what you know about them on a deeper level. Here we're looking for insights into the target audience that will help us develop our story so that it will be compelling to them specifically.

Going back to the conversation analogy, it's much easier to engage someone in conversation once you know a bit about them. You can look at the world through their eyes and tell your story in a way that will be meaningful to them, which may or may not be the same as what's meaningful to you.

Target audience insights explore how people think, feel and behave around your category, brand and product.

Some of the nuts and bolts in this element can include:

- Frequency of purchase
- Purchase decision-maker and influencers
- Repertoire/switching behaviour
- Brand and product usage patterns
- Level of commitment and involvement
- Key barriers to purchase
- Key drivers of brand selection and brand satisfaction

## Group 2 – What Do You Do?

This next section builds on the clear view of who you're talking to, as summarised in Group 1. It provides a concise summary of the key elements of what the brand has to offer. It goes from very tangible to quite abstract.

In the Nutshell model, it is the upper left hand point of the triangle, as illustrated below.

Like the first part of the model, there are three elements of a brand positioning that make up this part:

- Attributes
- Functional Benefits
- Emotional End Benefits

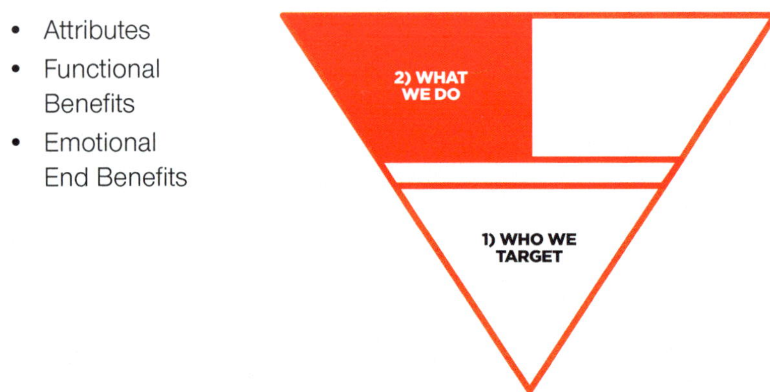


## Attributes

Attributes are the physical, tangible, observable building blocks of the product or service that the brand represents.

Think of a laundry soap. Its attributes might be that it is a powder, it contains a patented enzyme, it is biodegradable, etc. These attributes, or features, are the building blocks that help the product do what it does, but they tend to be a means to an end, rather than the whole reason to buy the product. They certainly won't be the whole story of the brand.

## Functional Benefits

If the attributes of a brand are the building blocks of the product or service, the functional benefit is the practical job that the brand does.

For example, the laundry detergent mentioned above makes white clothes whiter. The functional benefit is 'makes white clothes whiter'. Its patented enzyme is the key attribute that drives the functional benefit of making whites whiter.

As you can see, we're still in very rational, pragmatic territory here. We're only talking about what the brand does in functional terms, not how it does it or why, or how it makes the customer feel. That comes next.

## Emotional End Benefit

I call this, the 'so what' factor. The questions that need to be asked here are:

Q   How does the target audience feel when they buy/use the brand?

Q   What's in it for the target audience to choose/use the brand?

Q   What need is the brand fulfilling for the target audience?

Q   What does the target audience ultimately get out of their engagement with the brand – psychologically or emotionally?

It's really important that you capture the perspective of the target audience under this heading. This section is not about you or the product. It's about what the target audience gets out of it.

Back to the laundry detergent again. Because it makes white clothes whiter, users feel proud that they're taking good care of their family. The emotional end benefit might be pride, or satisfaction that you've done the best for your family.

There are no cookie-cutter answers here. Most products might have a wide range of benefits and will need to make a strategic decision about which one to leverage in their brand strategy. The laundry detergent example is a bit clichéd, but it is only meant to illustrate the difference between a functional benefit and an emotional end benefit.

In the movie 'When Harry Met Sally', there's a popular scene where Meg Ryan is trying to convince Billy Crystal that women can 'fake it' in bed. He doesn't believe her, so she proceeds to give him a very loud and convincing demonstration, sitting across from him in a crowded diner. He is mortified. An older woman at a nearby table (played by the director's mother, as it turns out!) delivers one of the most famous movie lines ever to her waiter: 'I'll have what she's having.'

In fact, the older woman has no idea what Meg Ryan had ordered. She wasn't basing her choice on the attribute, or even the functional benefit, of whatever Meg Ryan was eating. She wanted to **feel** what Meg Ryan was feeling and was happy to choose whatever dish was going to give her that feeling.

There's an important lesson in this. If you can offer an end benefit to your target audience in a way that is compelling, it can help you rise above the details of the tangible attributes of your brand. Tangible attributes can sometimes be copied by your competitors, can be superseded by innovations, and generally drag down your story to the rational. Taking the high ground like this can help you to avoid price wars and minimise the risk of limiting yourself and your brand.

If you're selling an end benefit, you can stretch your brand into new attributes and a range of functional benefits, even new products, without losing focus and clarity for the brand.

## Group 3 – Who Are You?

The model is starting to take shape now. In this next grouping, the goal is to capture what makes your brand tick and help your target audience get to know your brand on a more human level.

Group 3 only contains two elements:

- Brand Personality
- Brand Values/ Drivers

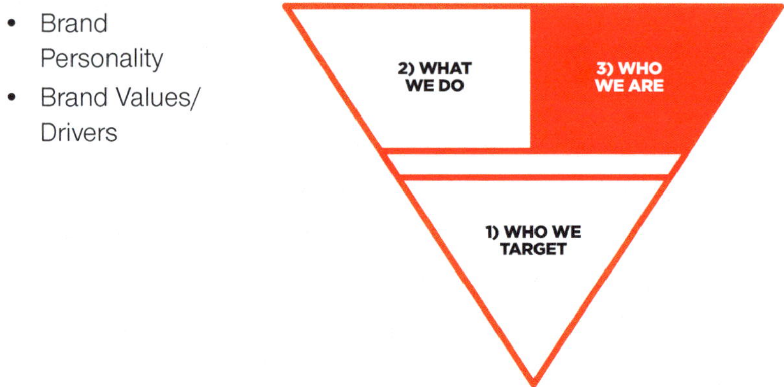


So far in the model, we've explored 'who' you target and 'what' you do, including the 'so what' factor. In this section, we explore the 'how' factor and the 'why' factor.

## Brand Personality

Brand Personality is the 'how' factor.

How you do what you do can be as important as the product or service you offer. Think about what happens when you meet someone new. In a group of people, or even from a distance, you take in certain information about a person and form an impression of them. Tall or short, blond or brunette, brown eyes or blue, short hair or long, untidy or neat, formally or casually dressed, fit or out of shape, etc. These are some of their attributes, the tangible, physical, observable characteristics that they exhibit. But you'd hardly say you know the person yet, based on these attributes.

Next, you might get the chance to meet and have a conversation. Their voice is another attribute that may make some sort of impression on you. But how they talk and express themselves, how they behave and interact with other people, how they carry themselves, these are elements that start to give you a sense of their personality. When you have a sense of their personality, then you start to form an opinion about what sort of person this is.

It's the same with brands. There are all sorts of cues from a brand that give us a sense of what its personality is. Personality can be the tie-breaking factor that works in a brand's favour, particularly in a category that's crowded with options, or one where the target audience doesn't care enough to do lots of research to work out which option is rationally superior.

Although it sounds a bit abstract, a brand will always have a personality, even if it might be 'bland', so it's important to work through what the right personality is for your brand, so that it can be correctly and consistently reflected in everything the brand does and in every opportunity it has to come in contact with your target audience.

This can be a difficult aspect to work through, because it feels quite abstract to some people. But don't worry, by the time you get to Chapter 11 and start writing your brand positioning, you will have received plenty of tips and tools to work through it in a practical way.

## Brand Values/Drivers

This is often the trickiest part of the model to complete, perhaps because it's so prone to clichés and motherhood statements.

Remember, you're trying to help your target audience get to understand your brand and to connect with it, so you want to include things that are insightful and revealing about what makes your brand tick.

I call this the 'Why' factor. Why does the brand do what it does? What are the drivers and motivators that, metaphorically, get the brand out of bed in the morning and go in to work every day? What are the principles and philosophies that underpin the decisions the brand makes on how to behave and what it wants to contribute and achieve? What is your brand's purpose? What are its core beliefs?

Simon Sinek has become very well know in strategy circles for a model he calls the Golden Circle, which focuses on the 'why' factor. He explains it clearly and powerfully in a TED talk called 'How Great Leaders Inspire Action' that you can find on YouTube.

## Group 4 – The Core Promise

Okay, this isn't a grouping at all. It only has a single element in it, but it's arguably the most important element of all.

The core promise brings the whole story to a focus.

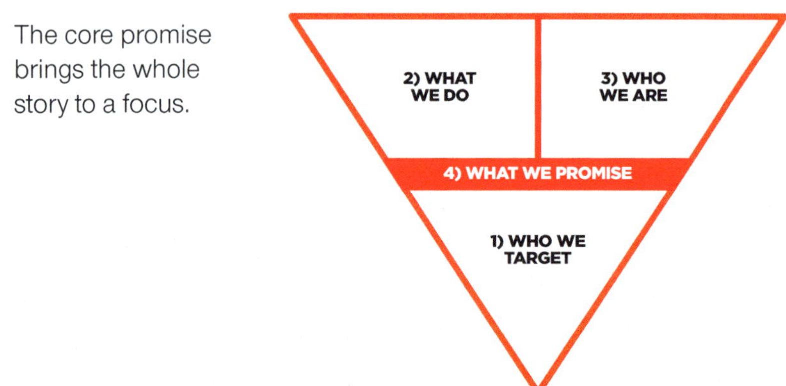


We've nearly completed the discussion of the model now. We've described the target audience of the brand, providing the point on which the story of the brand balances. From there, we added the summary of what we do for the target audience. Then we rounded it out with a summary of how we want to be perceived by the target audience on a more human level – the brand's personality and its drivers.

We now have all of the major component parts of the brand positioning. What's left is to articulate the essence of it in a concise, unambiguous phrase or sentence. That's the core promise of the brand.

When the core promise is well written, it is a concise statement summarising the story you want to tell about your brand, captured in a sentence. It sits in the middle of the model to visually communicate that it is the heart of the story.

## An Example – The Nutshell Model for the Nutshell Brand

Before we move on to process, let me share the brand summary for my business – Nutshell Brand Consultancy. This finished example should help to bring the whole model to life.

In developing my brand positioning, I started by creating a portrait for myself of the types of clients I felt I could help the most, not to mention the ones I derive the most satisfaction from helping.

Then I worked through the attributes and benefits I had to offer. It's worth noting that the attributes provide credibility and are good reasons to believe my promise, but they take a back seat and are not the promise itself.

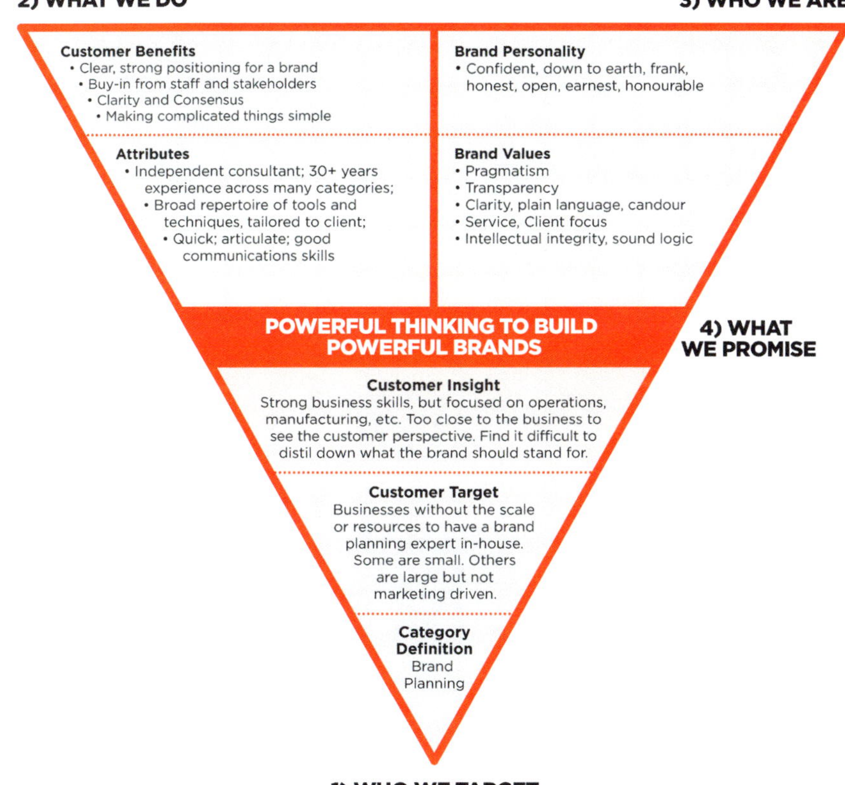

The key words that I circled in my brand summary triangle in order to get to my core promise were:

- Businesses without the resources to focus on marketing
- Clarity and consensus
- Pragmatism
- Plain language
- Service, helping clients to achieve their objectives
- Intellectual integrity
- Sound logic
- Frank, open, honest

You'll also notice that words from the Brand Personality box and the Brand Values box feature prominently in my list of highlighted words. This reflects that it's **how** I do what I do and **why** I do it that set me apart. They are not lofty and saint-like, but I believe they resonate with the sorts of clients I hope to attract and set the tone for how I offer to work with clients and add value to their organisation.

You might even notice that the business name, Nutshell, is a reflection of the brand positioning. This is how it should be. If you have a brand positioning that is well thought out and genuinely captures the essence of what you have to offer, it should be reflected in everything the brand says and does.

# PART TWO
# PUTTING THEORY INTO PRACTICE

This part of *Brand Positioning in a Nutshell* guides you through a practical, pragmatic process of implementing the theory in the first part of the book, to unlock the positioning of your brand.

**CHAPTER 5**

# THE PROCESS OVERVIEW

Now it's time to take all the concepts discussed in this book up to here and start to put them into practice specifically for your brand.

The Nutshell process involves five simple steps that provide a clear, logical approach to developing the positioning you need to guide the long-term success of your brand.

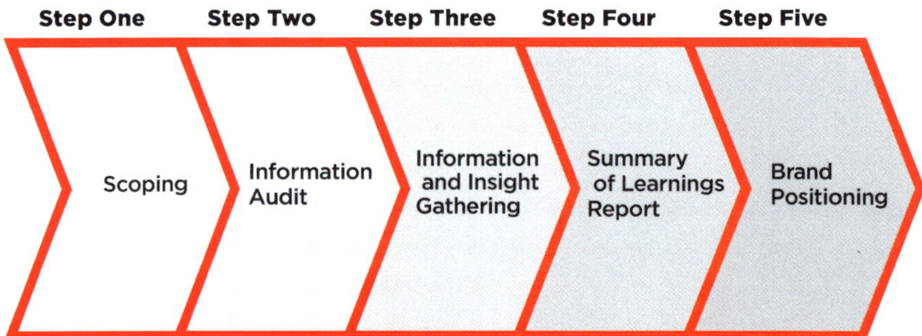


## STEP ONE – SCOPING

| Objectives | <ul><li>Confirm category definition</li><li>Review desired outcomes for the business</li><li>Determine key stakeholders and target audiences</li></ul> |
|---|---|
| Outputs | Top line project plan |

In Step One, all you need to do is summarise the big picture of where you want your brand to be and who will be involved in getting it there.

Once you've done that, you've got the context for working through the remaining four steps.

## STEP TWO – INFORMATION AUDIT 

| | |
|---|---|
| Objectives | • Review all existing relevant information<br>• Identify information gaps<br>• Develop plan to fill information gaps where necessary and possible |
| Outputs | Detailed plan for gathering information and insights |

Step Two starts with a list of information that is helpful in the process of developing a sound brand positioning. It also works through what to do if you don't have all the information, which is often the case and never the end of the world, so don't panic.

## STEP THREE – RESEARCH AND ENGAGEMENT 

| | |
|---|---|
| Objectives | • Gain insights into how customers and prospects think, feel and behave around the category and the brand.<br>• Gather perspectives of key internal stakeholders about their vision for the business and the brand<br>• Gather perspectives of key external stakeholders on their perceptions, expectations and desires of the business and brand<br>• Review competitors |
| Outputs | Forms part of the Summary of Learnings report |

Step Three is about getting you outside of your own head and making sure that you build your brand positioning on a strong foundation from the people who will buy it and the people who will make it work. It's the key to making sure your positioning provides deliverability, differentiation and desirability in the brand strategy trifecta.

## STEP FOUR – SUMMARY OF LEARNINGS 

| | |
|---|---|
| Objectives | • Ensure that internal stakeholders are on the same page in terms of the key observations and insights that will inform the brand positioning recommendation |
| Outputs | Report |

Step Four gives you time to pause, gather together everything you've learned up to this point and put it all in one report in an organised way. It's where the answer begins to emerge.

## STEP FIVE – BRAND POSITIONING 

| | |
|---|---|
| Objectives | Ensure clarity and consensus on the direction for the brand |
| Process/Activities | Positioning development |
| Outputs | The one-page Nutshell Brand Positioning summary and supporting rationale |

This is where the magic happens. You take everything you've learned and structure it into the format of the Nutshell brand positioning model. Here is where all your hard work pays off and you experience the big 'Aha' moment where it all makes sense.

# CHAPTER 6

# STEP ONE – SCOPING

| Alice: | 'Would you tell me, please, which way I ought to go from here?' |
|---|---|
| Cheshire Cat: | 'That depends a good deal on where you want to get to.' |
| Alice: | 'I don't much care where –' |
| Cheshire Cat: | 'Then it doesn't matter which way you go.' |

Lewis Carroll, Alice in Wonderland

I'm going to assume you care a great deal about where you go from here and that you understand the circular model for managing a brand presented in Chapter 3, especially the notions of 'Where are we?' and 'Where could we be?'.

Remember, this book doesn't set out to tell you where you should go — it helps guide you through the things you need to work out as a foundation for positioning your brand, so that you get to where you want to be.

## BUSINESS OBJECTIVES AND STRATEGY

Use your workbook (pages 5–7) to work through a concise overview of your business strategy. Don't worry about answering all the questions in great detail, but you need to get fairly specific with your business objectives at least at a big picture level as context for writing your brand strategy.

| | CURRENT | MEDIUM TERM | LONG TERM |
|---|---|---|---|
| Product | What are you selling now? | What additional products are you currently working on that could be launched within the next year or two? | Thinking really big picture, what is the complete list of products that you could imagine your brand offering? |

| | CURRENT | MEDIUM TERM | LONG TERM |
|---|---|---|---|
| Category Definition | How do you define what business you're in now? What heading would someone find you under in the Yellow Pages? What would they search for on the internet? | As you add products, does your category definition change? Are you in a broader category? | In the big picture scenario, what's the broadest category where you see yourself competing? Would it be clearer to list a few categories that you would ultimately compete in? |
| Target Audience | Who is currently buying your products? | What additional target markets could you sell to with your existing products and/or new products available in the medium term? | In the big picture scenarios above, who would be buying the range of products you imagine your brand offering? |
| Competitors | What other products are your customers considering as an alternative to yours? What are they buying instead of your product? | As you add products, are there other brands that become competitors? Which ones? | If you expanded your brand offer as far as you could imagine, who would be your competitors then? |
| Sales: Volume/ Share | What are your sales (in dollars and/or units) now?<br><br>What's your market share? | What are your sales and market share objectives for the next 1, 2 and 3 years? | What about in 10 years? |

| | CURRENT | MEDIUM TERM | LONG TERM |
| --- | --- | --- | --- |
| Source of Growth<br><br>1. Increased sales to existing customers<br>2. New customers<br>3. New distribution channels<br>4. New products | n/a | How will each of these sources of growth contribute to the growth you're after for your brand, based on the answers to all the questions in this grid so far? | Will the relative importance of these various sources of growth change as you get closer to the ultimate objectives you have for your brand? If so, how? |

It's important to position your brand for where you want to be, not just where you are now.

A brand positioning is meant to guide everything a brand does towards its goals, so by implication the positioning should be relevant to a reasonably long-term time frame. If you have to reposition your brand every time you launch a new product or go after a new target audience, it will be hard to establish a clear understanding of your brand in the minds of your target audience and stakeholders.

## CATEGORY DEFINITION

We need to go into some more detail and actually define your category before we proceed. Defining what category you're in is fundamental to scoping the project and everything else about developing a brand positioning, so we can't defer it till later.

There's no definitive source to tell you what to call the category you're in, but you do want to use whatever names are most commonly used to define your category. Remember that the purpose of defining your category is to be clear about your competition and your target audience (and what they want). That frames up the conversation you need to have with your prospects to get them to choose your brand.

There's no right or wrong answer, but deciding what business you see yourself as being in can have major implications for your brand positioning.

A travel agent might be in the business of booking flights, researching options to create the travel itinerary that's right for you, or helping your holiday dreams to come true.

Similarly, a laundry detergent might be in the business of manufacturing laundry soap, cleaning clothes, helping people make a good impression, or helping homemakers feel like they're taking the best possible care of their families. It depends on how that detergent brand wants to define itself in the minds of its target audience.

You might say that all the answers to 'what business are you in?' for each of the examples above are right. I wouldn't disagree. But where it is most important is in how it sets up who you want to talk to, the contents of the conversation you want to have, and even who your competition would be for the attention of your target audience.

If you're in the business of manufacturing nail polish, you compete only with other nail polish manufacturers. To compete effectively, you need to explain to customers why they should buy your nail polish over a competitor's.

If you're in the cosmetics business, you compete with every other company selling lipsticks, lip gloss, mascara, eyeliner, eye shadow, foundation, cleansers, moisturisers, etc.

If you're in the business of selling beauty, you compete with all the above, plus hair colour, beauty salons, spas, plastic surgery, and probably lots of other things.

As your category definition becomes broader, you increase the size of the opportunity you can potentially pursue, but you also increase the number and diversity of competitors you will take on.  At the same time, you decrease your focus and your ability to clearly and succinctly define what makes you different in an ownable way. It's a balancing act that every organisation must work out for itself.

Make sure you're thinking in terms of your long-term business strategy, to make sure you are defining the category you ultimately want to be in, just in case that turns out to be different to the category you are in now.

If you're not already absolutely clear on your category definition, you can explore it a bit further by using the following prompts. You want to try to get this down to just a simple, one or two word name for the category, to put the rest of the brand positioning in context.

**Q**  What would an everyday person call the category your brand is in?

**Q**  What's your most straightforward answer when someone asks 'what business are you in'?

**Q**  Under what heading would someone find you in the Yellow Pages?

**Q**  What Google search term would be most likely to find you and your key competitors?

## TARGET AUDIENCE AND STAKEHOLDERS

Now you're ready to work through who's going to help your business achieve its long-term goals in its designated category.

I almost always start the brand positioning process with a new client by asking two simple questions. The answers provide the key to setting up the project for a successful outcome, so it's important to explore them both thoroughly.

| |
|---|
| **Whose perceptions of the organisation/ Brand matter?** |

| |
|---|
| **Who needs to support the brand positioning?** |

## Whose perceptions of the brand matter?

If you continue the analogy of thinking about brand positioning as the story for your brand, the answer to this question is found by exploring who the brand needs to tell its story to, in order to be successful.

It's not enough to say 'people who might buy my product'.  Of course, the purchaser is an important target audience, but you need to think through everyone whose positive perceptions of your brand will contribute to your success.

For example, think about an organisation running a major event in a city. The event brings lots of people and attention to the city and dominates a venue or an area for a period of time. It might be a concert, a festival, a sporting event, etc.

Thinking that through, the list of people whose perceptions of the brand matter could include:

- Ticket buyers
- Local residents
- Musicians (or athletes, or delegates, etc)
- Volunteers
- Sponsors

- Schools and/or universities
- Local businesses
- Local sporting clubs
- Tourists and visitors (who might be further broken down by whether they are from within driving distance or further, domestic vs. international, etc)

You want to make a list comprehensive enough to identify any group that might require a conversation that's specific to that group. Obviously, you'd have a different conversation with the people who were going to participate in your event (like musicians or athletes) than you would with school children or local businesses or local residents.

Your list of target audiences might not be as complex as this example, but make sure you think it through thoroughly.

 Use your workbook (pages 8–9) to list the various target audiences that come to mind for your brand.

## Who needs to support the brand positioning?

Let's assume this is day one of the process of you working through creating a brand positioning. My first piece of advice is, don't take the project on your shoulders alone.

Who else, besides yourself, will be critical to living the brand positioning in order to drive its success? Think about what departments or functional areas, such as manufacturing, sales, operations, HR, management, etc, should be involved in order to achieve consensus and therefore consistent execution of the brand positioning. Think in terms of divisions or silos within the organisation, such as headquarters, field offices, project teams, product teams, etc.

One way to start is to get out a copy of your organisational chart. Ask yourself:

Q  How many people are there in the different boxes in the chart?

Q  What is the interaction between different groups in the chart?

Q  How well do the different groups collaborate with one another?

Q  How influential is each group in the chart in terms of gaining support internally for initiatives the business wants to undertake?

Q  How well are the different groups in touch with your target audience?

Q  What role does each group play in representing or living the brand to external audiences?

Q  What role does each group play in empowering the brand to deliver on what it promises?

Any group that plays a significant role in making sure the organisation lives up to its brand positioning should be engaged in the process of developing the positioning.

It's about **consensus**. Designing a brand positioning project optimally means including all relevant perspectives on what the brand story should be, so that when the brand story is finalised, everyone is one board and committed to it. If you find yourself thinking that particular groups in the organisation will be hard to convince or won't agree with other parts, don't fall into the trap of trying to keep them out of the process to make things easier. In the end, it will only make things harder because they will potentially undermine the brand positioning or minimise its effectiveness by going off in different directions, resulting in an inconsistent or unclear delivery of the positioning. You need to stay open to the perspective of all key internal stakeholders to make this work.

Next, start thinking about specific individuals in each of the groups on the organisational chart. If you don't feel like you personally know enough of the people in each group, work out your best contact within the organisation to give you a detailed perspective on the people in each group.

What you're looking for is a list of the most influential individuals in each group. Think of them as the opinion leaders in their area. I often describe them as the 'alpha individuals' in their area. They are the people who others around them seek out for their opinions and who are most highly considered or respected by the people they work with.

That doesn't mean they are necessarily the most senior or the most highly paid. In many organisations, the receptionist or the office manager is an iconic person who is a living symbol of what the organisation is all about. The people you're looking for are the ones who are known for their commitment to the organisation and their reflection of its values. You want the people who will bring others along with them if they buy in to the story for the brand.

Ultimately, you want to involve the smallest number of the most influential people in the organisation. You probably can't involve everyone, unless you're a very small organisation or a start-up, so you want to choose people whose support will carry the most weight, either formally or informally, with the most people.

Now, step outside the organisation. There may be other stakeholders who are critical to the organisation's ability to live its brand positioning.

This could include board members, government, industry groups, unions, suppliers, investors, media, etc. These are groups who are outside your control in a literal or organisational sense, but whose buy-in and support is important for you to be able to deliver on your core promise as a brand. Again, you may need to get input from colleagues and other people around you in the organisation to get it right. And don't forget, it's about identifying the smallest number of the most influential people.

Use the workbook (pages 9–14) to list the groups that you think you need to include in the process in order to achieve meaningful consensus. Then list the people you need to consult with to identify the right participants. That will be enough to help you develop a list of stakeholders for your brand positioning development process, which you can then also capture in the worksheet.

I have done projects with as few as two stakeholders and as many as several hundred. Don't be concerned yet with how many you identify, because there are ways to manage the process. We'll go into those later. It's more important to identify the right people than it is to limit it to a particular number.

# STEP TWO – INFORMATION AUDIT

This step is simply to review the availability of relevant information that already exists about the business and to review information gaps. You don't have to collect it yet. It's just about preparing an overview of what is available.

Here's the wish list that I start with for my clients.

## The Category
- Category Definition
- Size (in units and/or $)
- Growth trends (over last 5 years and projected for the next 5 years)
- Rate of change and innovation
- Level of differentiation amongst competitors

## The Business
- History
- Organisational structure
- Size (in units and/or $)
- Market share
- Business objectives (short and long term)
- Product/service description
- Pricing
- Strengths and Weaknesses
- Opportunities and Threats
- Current Brand Positioning
- Marketing and Communications materials

## Competitors
- Market share
- Positioning of key competitors
- Pricing of key competitors
- Strengths and weakneses of key competitors
- Marketing and communications materials of key competitors

## The Consumer/Customer
- Demographic description
  - Gender
  - Age
  - Income
  - Occupation
  - Employment Status
  - Education

- – Ethnic or Cultural Background
- – Life Stage
- – Geography
- – Core vs. Secondary Target Audience
- Attitudes and Behaviour regarding the category and individual brands
  - – Frequency of purchase
  - – Purchase decision-maker and influencers
  - – Key drivers of brand selection and satisfaction
  - – Repertoire/switching behaviour
  - – Usage patterns
  - – Level of commitment/involvement
  - – Key barriers to purchase
  - – Key drivers of brand selection and brand satisfaction

Some of the information will be at your fingertips. Make a note to collect it and bring it all together in one place for this process.

Other items might not be to hand, but will be available through someone else in your organisation or through an external source. Make a note of the source of the information and the cost (if any) and time involved in acquiring it.

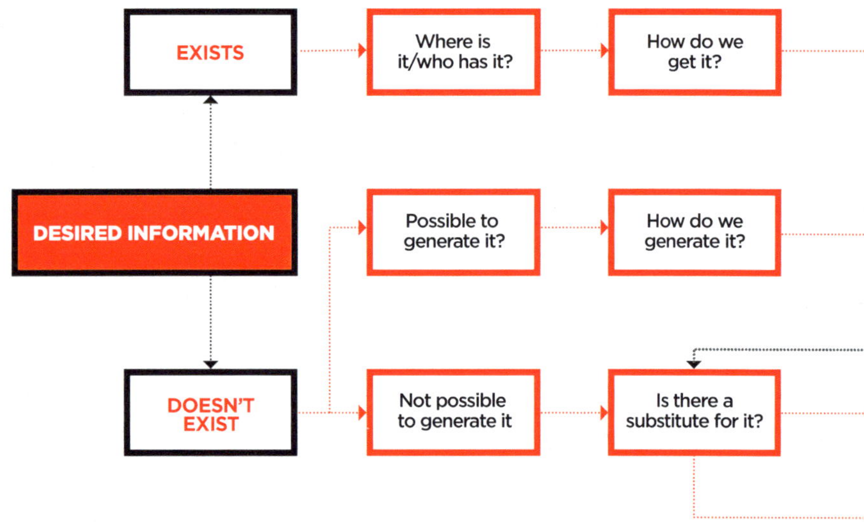

There may be other items in the wish list that aren't currently available at all. For those, the first step is to think about whether there is a useful proxy that is available, or whether you can use experience and judgment to make an informed guess that will be accurate enough for the purposes of this process.

If you can't use existing information as a proxy or make an educated guess, think about how you might acquire the information, through some sort of research or data collection, depending on what the information gap is. Make a note about the estimated cost and timing involved in collecting the missing information if you can. Otherwise the next chapter includes a section on ways to fill various information gaps.

Armed with the estimates of cost and timing for collecting the missing information, you need to make a judgment call on whether it's worth it to you to fill a particular gap. It comes down to how big a compromise you think there will be in terms of developing a story for your brand without that information and how much better/more effective you will be able to make your story as a result of having specific information available.

At the risk of making this seem like an engineering project, the following diagram represents this process of working through the wish list of information.

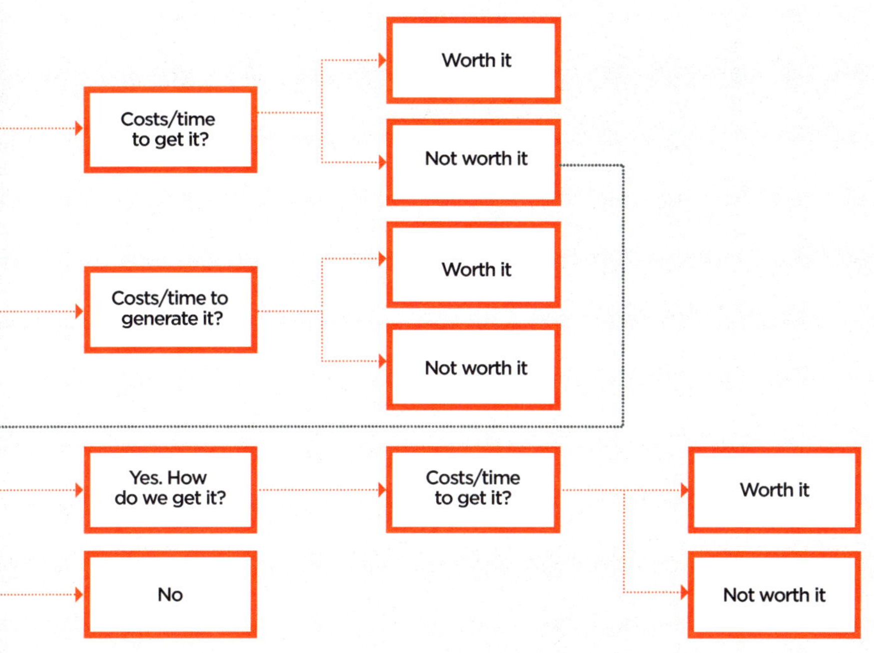

The only items that I consider essential to have full information for in this list are:

- Category definition – Clarity on your competitive frame is essential to working through the story you need to tell about your brand. Without it, you really don't know what you're trying to have a conversation about with your customer.
- Target Audience – You need to have a clear mental image of your customer, in order to have an effective conversation with them.
- Business – You need to be confident about what your business can and can't do before you start articulating the promise you want your brand to make.

It's okay to use gut instinct as a basis for completing the information audit, if you're confident in your instincts. It's better to trust your instincts, make decisions, go out there and do something and learn from it, than to spend ages collecting data and never take action.

You're the best one to judge how confident you are in your instincts and whether you need reassurance about your assumptions.

When you finish the audit, you will have completed a summary sheet that includes a list of all the key information from the wish list and your bottom-line assessment of the availability of that information. That will be your reference when you start gathering the information in the next chapter.

 Use your workbook (pages 15–19), to capture your thoughts on the information audit.

# STEP THREE – INFORMATION AND INSIGHT GATHERING

Now we can gather the information and insights that will drive your brand positioning.

The first part of this chapter talks about sources of key business and consumer information that you will need in order to develop your brand positioning. The second part goes into detail on how to engage with stakeholders and customers in order to collect information you don't already have and to do it in such a way that you achieve clarity and consensus in your end result.

When we went through the information audit overview in the previous chapter, you made notes about what information was available, what wasn't available and whether there was alternative information you could access if necessary.

That audit is the starting point for this step in the process. Working from the grid that you completed in the previous chapter (pages 15–19 in your workbook), start by physically collecting all the information that you marked as being currently available. Then organise it in individual folders according to the headings in the audit:

- Category
- The Business
- Competitors
- The Customer/Consumer

Don't worry about editing down the information at this stage. For the time being, we're just collecting all the information that will potentially be relevant.

Continuing to refer to the grid you created in Chapter 6, there will undoubtedly be information that would be useful but is not currently in your possession.  Let's work our way through the sort of information you will be looking to collect and how you can get it.

 Use your workbook (pages 20–36) to help capture key information.

## CATEGORY

### Category Dynamics

If you found, in the information audit stage, that you were missing key information about the category and you don't feel entirely comfortable using your own judgement to estimate the answers, it's time to search through information that might be available publicly or for a price.

There are many sources that you can explore with a simple internet search, including:

- Industry analysis reports from companies like IBIS, that syndicate their information. Typically, you need to pay for these reports, but sometimes you can find topline summaries that are publicly available.
- Industry associations in your category
- Government departments, for census information, etc.
- Universities
- Overseas information about the same category in other countries
- Case studies from research companies or competitors

If you can't find information that definitively answers the questions in the audit, you'll probably want to use your best guess or consult with any contacts you have for their best guesses. It's likely to be prohibitively expensive to conduct market research or collect enough data yourself to quantify the answers from scratch.

## THE BUSINESS

The information on the business, its strategies and objectives, will need to come from you and any relevant internal stakeholders.

If you were able to tick 'available' for all the headings under 'business' in the information audit grid in Chapter 6, it should just be a matter of gathering the information you listed and adding it to your collection for the first part of this list. Your folder under the heading of 'The Business' will have the following headings and you should now be able to add the information that fleshes out the detail under each of the headings.

### Business Overview
- Business history
- Current state of the business
- Business objectives
- Product overview
- Current brand positioning
- Marketing and communications materials

If you don't have all the information readily available, you may be able to work with other people in the organisation to get it. It may require help from the finance department or bookkeepers to analyse sales and revenue figures, working with the sales and/or marketing departments to identify key competitors, strengths and weaknesses, etc.

## COMPETITORS

Industry information that you've gathered may contain references to key players in the category, which can help you identify competitors if you're not already clear on who they would be.

To learn more about the brands you consider competitors, start with the obvious things like downloading their annual reports from the internet, reading their websites and searching for articles or mentions about them on the internet. In addition to that, it's useful to talk about how your target audience and stakeholders perceive your competitors, which you can do during the stakeholder engagement process.

- Name the three brands you consider your most significant competitors:
- Now briefly explain why you consider them key competitors:
- For each of your three key competitors, you're looking for information on their
    - Market share
    - Pricing
    - Strengths and weaknesses
    - Key attributes and functional benefits
    - Consumer needs they are addressing
    - Personality and values of their brands
    - Their core promise/what they offer their customers

Going through this process will help you assess the strength and level of differentiation of your brand positioning.

## THE CUSTOMER/CONSUMER

If you have an existing business, you may already have a fair bit of information on your customers and prospects.

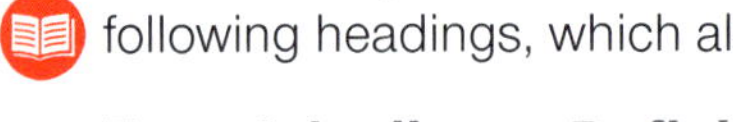

Start with any relevant information you have and organise it under the following headings, which also appear in your workbook (pages 29–30).

### Target Audience Definition
    - Gender
    - Age
    - Income
    - Occupation
    - Employment status
    - Education
    - Ethnic or Cultural Background

- Life Stage
- Geography

**Target Audience Insights**

- Frequency of Purchase
- Purchase decision-maker and influences
- Repertoire/Switching behaviour
- Brand and product usage patterns
- Level of commitment and involvement with brands
- Key barriers to purchase
- Key drivers of brand selection and brand satisfaction

Supplement the information you have with anything you can learn from the various information sources listed on page 64 under 'category dynamics'.

 If there are still information gaps that you feel should be filled, read on to learn more about getting information and insights from research and stakeholders. As you gather insights, capture them in your workbook on pages 31–36.

## RESEARCH AND ENGAGEMENT TIPS AND TECHNIQUES

Here we will review methodologies for getting information from your customers, prospects and stakeholders directly.

We will build on your answers to the two key questions posed in Chapter 6:

Q   Whose perceptions of the brand matter?

Q   Who needs to support the brand positioning?

### Stakeholder Engagement

The list you developed for those who need to buy in to the brand positioning identifies your key stakeholders. I aim to engage with key stakeholders in enough detail that when I come back with a recommended brand positioning, they each recognise the contribution they made to the thinking that led to the recommendation.

With stakeholders, you are looking to explore the vision for the brand in terms of the nine component parts of the Nutshell Brand Positioning model. You want to get inside their heads and understand their thoughts on who the brand targets, what its key attributes are, what it does for consumers on a functional and emotional level and who the brand is in terms of personality and drivers/values.

In terms of the Brand Positioning Trifecta introduced in Chapter 3, this is an exploration of what the brand does or could **deliver**. We'll compare this to what the competitors deliver, as summarised on the previous page, in order to determine what **differentiates** your brand. Then we'll compare it to what the customer **desires**, which you'll explore in your target audience engagement process.

This engagement process can be done in a number of different ways, depending on the number of people on the list, their seniority, their accessibility and the groups/functions they represent.

The three main techniques I use are:

- One-on-one interviews
- Group workshops
- Surveys

**One-on-one interviews** are essential for the most senior people amongst your stakeholders. Typically, these people are important to their organisations, their opinion carries a great deal of weight and, whether they necessarily admit it or not, they expect their direction to be followed by those around them. If they don't feel they've been consulted and heard, there is a significant risk that they will not support the recommendations that come out of the process.

I find it invaluable to conduct these interviews one-on-one, because as soon as other stakeholders are present, a different dynamic arises where the interviewees either defer to one another or they jockey for position and dominance in the conversation. Either way, you lose the opportunity to establish a rapport and get a candid perspective from the stakeholder.

For similar reasons, I have a strong preference for conducting these conversations face-to-face. While it is possible to conduct them by phone, you lose the ability to read the subtle cues from the interviewee that can help you understand what they really think and guide the discussion to deeper, more meaningful levels.

Speaking as someone who is nearly always an outsider to the organisation represented by the interviewee, I find it important to strike a delicate balance by doing my homework beforehand and being a blank slate ready to record the thoughts and perspectives of the interviewee.

You need to know enough to demonstrate that you can keep up with the conversation and understand the points your interviewee is making, but at the end of the day your primary objective is to learn what they think, not tell them what you know or make recommendations to them. It's a fine art, something you get better at with practice. The key is to demonstrate your interest in what the interviewee has to say and to listen actively and respectfully.

Related to the idea of active listening is the balance between having an agenda for the interview and being willing and able to move away from the agenda if the conversation flows in a productive but unplanned direction.

Most busy, senior people will expect an agenda to be provided before an interview of this nature. It is a symbol of your respect for the interviewee to provide one. It also allows them the opportunity to prepare for the conversation, if they choose to, as well as providing reassurance that they will not be caught off guard by any lines of questioning you want to follow. Senior people (like most people) do not appreciate being seen as unprepared or inarticulate when asked for their professional opinion. In the case of very senior people, they may need time to get a briefing from some of their own staff, or pull together some information to feel fully prepared for the interview.

Having said that an agenda is important, I should also say that only a tiny minority of the interviews I have ever conducted proceeded according to a strict agenda. The underlying principle of the interview is that you don't know what you don't know, so it's important to be prepared to pick up on things the interviewee says and follow where the conversation leads, thinking on your feet and engaging in a genuine conversation rather than a sterile question and answer session.

One useful technique I use to manage the flow of the conversation is to identify something that I think is a key point from the interviewee, acknowledge it explicitly ('That sounds like a really important point to me' or 'That feels like a key point. Can we talk about that a little more?'), and then try to re-state what they've said ('If I understand correctly what you're saying, then…' or 'Am I right in understanding that you're saying that…'). By doing this, you reinforce that you have understood the point being made and underscore the fact that the interviewee has contributed something important to the thinking. Also, if by chance you didn't get it right, the interviewee has the opportunity to explain in more detail and you ensure that you do in fact understand the point being made.

Similarly, I try to summarise the key points the interviewee has made before I finish the interview. After that, I nearly always ask a final, open-ended question about whether there is anything else they feel I should know, in order to achieve a success outcome to the project I'm undertaking.

The reality is that the interviewees have been selected because they have a valuable perspective on the topic, so you should never be afraid to make it clear that you're learning from them and find their perspective valuable.

**Workshops** can be used when there are more people who need to be part of the process than you can realistically meet with individually.

The group that participates in a workshop together needs to have some common ground. They can be from the same department, have shared goals, work together on a specific project or function, have a shared issue or challenge, etc. It can be as broad as working for the same organisation, but ideally they should have a little bit more of a shared perspective, so the conversation builds and goes deeper rather than focusing on differences.

Again, the purpose of the workshop is to gain an understanding of how this group of people view the brand, the target audience, the competition, the opportunities and challenges, etc, so that when a recommended brand positioning is presented back to the organisation, they see the merit in it and recognise their contribution.

Workshops work well with as few as six or eight people and can be successfully managed with as many as 20 or 25, though a few techniques need to be employed to manage larger numbers. Here are some tips on managing workshops.

I like to start workshops with a brief discussion of why the session has been booked and what I hope to accomplish in it. I always ask whether my objectives are consistent with the expectations and understanding they brought into the meeting, to make sure everyone's on the same page before we start. This is rarely an issue, because I try to ensure that an agenda has been issued at least a couple of days before the workshop.

In many cases, a bit of 'homework' or preparation is valuable before the workshop, along with some pre-reading on the background of the project being undertaken. This saves time in the meeting and allows us to jump straight into the topic and actively engages the participants rather than delivering presentations and reviewing background information.

Like stakeholder interviews, active listening and flexibility around the agenda are keys to successful workshops.

The specific techniques are slightly different, however.

The facilitator of a workshop like this has to make sure to record all key input from the group and make sure that everyone sees very clearly that they've been heard. A whiteboard can be your best friend in this situation. In fact, I often lighten the mood at the beginning of a workshop by admitting that printable whiteboards are my favourite thing (sad but true) and asking for the group's patience with my terrible hand-writing. These things give me the excuse to ask everyone to speak one at a time and make sure I capture what they've said so we don't miss anything.

Another similarity to stakeholder interviews is that I often take the opportunity to acknowledge what strikes me as a key point whenever one is made by someone in the group. I restate it, to make sure that I understood correctly and probe further if necessary. The difference in a workshop is that you also get to ask if others agree with the point or whether there are other perspectives to be explored.

I loop back to points made earlier when I see a connection with something someone says and get the group to talk more about it.

I (respectfully) challenge participants to be clear on what they're saying. I point out inconsistencies that I notice between what various people say, not to find fault but to understand what the dynamics are that allow apparent contradictions to coexist.

I do a lot of recapping and restating when I think I see patterns or key thoughts emerging, to reinforce them if they're right and correct my understanding if I got it wrong.

In large workshops, I always introduce an exercise that involves smaller breakout groups, towards the end of the session, when we're beginning to see the answers we're looking for. A good example is to work through the key building blocks of a brand positioning (category definition, target audience, brand attributes, functional benefits, end benefit, brand personality and brand drivers/values) as a group. All the building blocks except the core promise have now been covered. When we get to that point, having had a rich and engaged discussion, I split the room into groups of 3 or 4, depending on how many are in the workshop. If it's a small group, this can be an individual exercise.

I explain to the group that, when we finish the session, it's my job to go away and distil down what I've heard from them and all the other stakeholders I've spoken to into a clear concise summary of the promise for the brand. I also explain that writing something like that as a group is virtually impossible, because it becomes about finessing words rather than finding the core thought.

I then send them into their groups and ask them to come up with a simple sentence that, in plain language, articulates the core promise of the brand as it is emerging from the work we've done together in the workshop. I encourage them to forget about marketing language and corporate-speak and give them permission to be as imperfect or as clumsy as they need to be, since I'm only going to give them a few minutes to think about it.

I wander around the room, checking in with each of the groups to see how they're going with the task, answering any questions or complimenting them on the work they're doing.

When the time's up (rarely more than 5–10 minutes), I get each group to simply read aloud what they came up with to the whole group. No explanation. No set-up. No rationale. No presentation. No discussion. The spokesperson for each group just reads their sentence, one after the other.

I'm going to give you my biggest secret now.

Remember that the main objective of engaging with key stakeholders is to achieve consensus around the recommended direction for the brand. When all the groups have read out their sentences, I pause for a moment and then ask the group for their reactions to what they've just heard. Every single time I have ever done this, the general response from the group is 'We've all said pretty much the same thing, in different words'. Bingo! There's your consensus. I didn't have to convince them that I found the answer. They observe for themselves that they essentially agree.

If there happen to be any significant disparities in what the groups come up with, I have the opportunity to bring them up and put them on the table for discussion, to resolve any inconsistency. Either way, I end up with a significant foundation for consensus before I leave the workshop.

The other key to a successful outcome is the time that goes by between conducting the workshop and coming back with the recommendation. I explain that it's important to go back through what everyone said in the engagement process, plus all the other relevant information that has been gathered, including consumer research, where relevant.

By the time I come back with my recommendation, no one remembers the exact wording they came up with, but they do recognise the similarity and consistency between what I've written and the output of the workshop.

As long as you're able to remind people of what they contributed in the workshops and/or interviews and demonstrate how that guided the recommendation you're making, consensus is surprisingly easy to achieve.

The key is taking a genuine interest in what stakeholders are saying and trying to fit the pieces into a coherent whole, rather than trying to force a conclusion on them from input that they haven't embraced.

As you can imagine, it's good to do workshops like this after you've done some of your initial fact-finding and senior stakeholder engagement, so you're able to keep tangents or impractical directions from gaining momentum.

**Surveys** are my least favourite methodology for this, because I find them to be the least satisfying of any engagement technique.

The good news is that they are useful when you need to engage with a particularly large number of people. The downside is that it's hard to be open-ended and exploratory with them. For practical purposes, you tend to need to ask questions that can be answered with yes or no, rated with a sliding scale of 'agree' to 'disagree', or answered from a list of options. Open-ended questions (for example 'How would you describe the brand personality of the organisation?') are difficult to administer because you have to transcribe the full answer for each respondent and then manually search for similarities and differences in the responses, which is very time-consuming.

For that reason, you tend to use surveys when you have some specific theories, ideas, or strategic territories that you want to explore with a large group of people. If you've already conducted your one-on-one interviews and done a few workshops and are beginning to see where the project might be going, it can be useful to get a reaction from the wider stakeholder population to either confirm what you're thinking or give you a reality check.

Again, the most valuable aspect of doing surveys is as a step towards consensus. By doing a survey, you're sending a signal to everyone who was invited to participate that their views are important. When the recommendation comes out, they know that they have contributed and are more likely to support the recommended direction.

There are lots of tools around these days to help with surveys and particularly with analysing the results. Survey Monkey is probably the most popular and it is specifically designed to be user-friendly for people who don't have a research background. As long as you're clear about what you want to ask and have a list of respondents, including email addresses, you shouldn't have any trouble implementing a survey with one of these tools.

## Target Audience Engagement

This is like stakeholder engagement, but now you are looking to explore the perceptions of the target audience in terms of the nine component parts of the Nutshell Brand Positioning model. You want to get inside the target audience's heads and understand their thoughts on what the brand's key attributes are, what it does for consumers on a functional and emotional level and who the brand is in terms of personality and drivers/values.

In terms of the Brand Positioning Trifecta, comparing the results of the target audience engagement with the results of the stakeholder engagement helps you discover whether what the customer **desires** is aligned with what the brand **delivers** and whether there are any gaps between how stakeholders see the brand vs. how the target audience sees it.

A similar set of tools to those described above for stakeholder engagement is available for engaging with your target audience:

- One-on-one interviews
- Focus Groups
- Surveys

**One-on-one interviews** involve recruiting individuals who are representative of your target audience and having a detailed, exploratory conversation with them about your category, product, etc. These interviews tend to be the most unstructured and open-ended of the types of consumer research mentioned here. They tend to be used early on in a project, to get a broad understanding of the consumer context and to begin to form hypotheses for further exploration. Because they tend to be few in number, it's important to avoid the temptation of assuming that what you learn is statistically significant. In other words, you don't talk to 10 people and conclude that 50% of your target audience behaves in a particular way because 5 of the people you spoke to said a particular thing.

One-on-one interviews (also called depth interviews, for the reasons described above) provide the landscape of how people in your target audience think, feel and behave in your category. You need to go further in order to quantify how dominant various thoughts and feelings are amongst the population and what messages would be most relevant and compelling for your brand.

**Focus groups** are another qualitative methodology, meaning that they are used to gain insights into how people are thinking and feeling and **why** they think what they think, not to quantify how many people think a particular way.

Focus groups are good because they bring together a small group of people in your target audience and create a somewhat realistic experience where people will talk about your category or product while you listen. In fact, most focus group facilities have a room behind a 2-way mirror where you (if you're using a professional researcher to moderate the groups) can watch and listen without influencing the group.

This kind of research can be a very valuable reality check for organisations that assume that everyone is highly engaged with their category, well informed about it and spends a lot of time thinking rationally about it. It's often a real wake-up call to discover that customers don't really think very actively about the category at all.

This kind of research can give you a very good picture of the people you're trying to have a conversation with about your brand when you market it.

**Surveys** are generally intended to be quantitative research, meaning that they are designed to provide a tangible measurement of things like:

- **how many** people think, feel, or behave in a particular way
- **how strong** a particular belief or opinion is amongst the target audience
- **clusters** of attitudes, opinions or behaviours (market segments or niches)
- how various measures are **tracking over time**

Like the surveys discussed above for stakeholder engagement, it's important to be clear about what you want to learn and have a good set of hypotheses that you want to test. That's because, in a survey, people can only answer the questions you ask them. They can't go off on an interesting tangent or inspire a line of questioning that you spontaneously follow with them.

To put it in the context of the circular brand management model from Chapter 3, quantitative surveys are quite good at answering 'Where are we now', assuming that you can put specific parameters around it so that people can answer with a yes/no, or agree/disagree type of answer.

By measuring 'where we are now' periodically, you get a measure of whether you're moving the brand to 'where you want to be'.

## A note on bringing in the experts

The premise of this book is that you can develop a brand positioning yourself and I stand behind that promise. It is, however, worth mentioning a few reasons to consider bringing in outside help.

## Researchers

Market research is a tricky business and there is a good reason people pay expert qualitative and quantitative researchers to design and conduct research for them. You probably know the expression 'Garbage in. Garbage out.' When applied to research, it means that if the questions you ask are structured incorrectly, sequenced inappropriately, etc, results that look quite conclusive can actually be meaningless – or worse – misleading.

It's very tempting to assume that we understand how what our target audience is thinking and feeling about the category and the brand. Don't fall into the trap of thinking that all you need to do is tell them about your brand in order to motivate them to choose it. If possible, it's worth confirming what you think you know before you start spending significant money implementing a brand positioning that's based on assumptions.

When it comes to research, your most important job is to think through what you need to know and why. This will come from the exercise you did in Chapter 7 where you audited available information and developed a list of information gaps. From there, if you can, I would strongly recommend you find the money to pay an experienced researcher to help construct the methodology for getting you what you need, particularly if it involves getting insights from your target audience.

## Strategists

The other expertise you might want to consider is a strategic consultant. Some of the reasons businesses bring people like me into a project are:

- They're just too busy running the business to step back and work out how to tell their story in the most compelling way.
- The organisation is complex and it's like herding cats trying to get everyone on the same page
- Politics and corporate culture make it hard for them to get candid, open input from staff and other internal stakeholders
- They're closer to the business than they are to their consumers and need a fresh set of eyes on whether they're selling the business as well as they could be

I encourage you to try it yourself and I believe this book gives you the principles and tools to do it successfully, but it's good to know that there are people out there with specific expertise that can help you over any hurdles that you might encounter.

# STEP FOUR – SUMMARY OF LEARNINGS

At this point in the process, I want to encourage you to pause, step back and reflect on what you've learned by going through the information audit on your brand and filling in any information gaps.

I'm not suggesting procrastination – I think we all have our own special skills and techniques in that area already! I am, however, suggesting you take stock of what you've learned as a way of making the next step simpler and more effective.

There's a pretty good chance that you now have quite a mountain of information spread out on a table in front of you, or at least saved in files on your computer. If you're tempted to jump straight into drafting your brand positioning, this chapter will take you through a number of reasons why it's worth holding off and doing an interim summary of what you've learned first. It will also give you some tips on how to organise everything you've learned up till now in a way that will make writing your brand positioning easier.

## FOUR KEY REASONS FOR THE SUMMARY

### 1) Assemble

You are likely to have information from several different sources in several different documents, files and formats at this stage. The Summary of Learnings report is a good tool for bringing that all together into one consolidated document. It is essentially the full library of information you will draw on to write your brand positioning.

I find that the act of reviewing and assembling all the information into one document helps me get it all into my head, where I can start processing it and working it through, even subconsciously.

It's a bit like a painter preparing his work area by laying out all the paints and brushes in front of the canvas. He probably doesn't know for sure which colours he's going to use yet or in which combination, but the process of laying them all out in front of him creates a sense of order and structure, so he knows where to find the right paints when he's ready for them. I think there's also an element of inspiration, looking at the array of beautiful colours he's about to use and getting excited about the picture that will eventually emerge.

### 2) Organise

The summary of learnings report is an important opportunity to start organising your thinking before you sit down to write your brand positioning. The information you've collected is likely to be organised by source. You've probably got a file on sales trends, a file on competitor positioning and activity, a file with notes from conversations with stakeholders, etc. The trick is to organise the information you've gathered so that it starts to line up with how you need to use it.

Particularly with things like consumer research and stakeholder interviews, I often get out a set of highlighters (maybe it's because I like the painter analogy so much) and highlight all my files and reports. I assign a colour to each of the major headings from the brand positioning:

- Target Audience Insight
- Attributes
- Functional Benefit
- Emotional End Benefit
- Brand Personality
- Brand Values/Drivers

Then I go through all my notes and documentation, scanning for anything that falls into one of those categories and highlighting it accordingly. There's a feeling of reassurance and confidence that I get out of this exercise, because it makes me feel that the answer I'm looking for is in there somewhere, even if I haven't found it yet.

It also helps in the writing of the report. You're essentially grouping everything you've learned, by heading, into the long list of content for your report.

There are other headings you will want to use in your summary of learnings report, which I'll go through later in this chapter, but the content for them tends to be more obvious, like business objectives, history of the brand, etc – so I don't use the highlighting technique for them. Feel free to adapt it to use in any way that suits you.

## 3) Retain

There's a trap I often fall into, that this report helps me to avoid. Maybe it can help you too. I sometimes get over-confident in my own memory. When I'm in the middle of a project and have all the key information swimming around in my head waiting to settle into a clear pattern that can become a recommendation, I feel like I will always have that level of clarity on the details.

The reality is that I have a very limited memory. If I'm not using a set of information actively, it's very easy for that information to get lost in the maze of my mental filing cabinet, never to be found. Unless I have a clever librarian to help find it, of course. That's what this report is. It's a way to capture and organise everything you've learned up to this point for future reference, when it's no longer fresh in your mind.

It's also really valuable for others who will be interested in what you learned but didn't participate in the process with you. I try to write these reports in such a way that they can stand alone and give the reader a complete picture of the process so far. I try to imagine someone reading the report who has no background at all on the subject and write it to get them to an equal footing with me in terms of what I'm going to draw on to write the brand positioning. You might even find that the reader is you!

## 4) Gain Agreement

You'll recall from Chapter 2 that clarity and consensus are the two main outcomes I aim for in developing a brand positioning. The Summary of Learnings report plays a very valuable role in achieving consensus.

After yourself, the second most important target audience for the Summary of Learnings report is the key stakeholders you identified early on in the process.

I urge you to distribute your Summary of Learnings report to anyone who you listed in answer to the question 'Who needs to support the brand strategy to ensure consistent, correct execution?'

Better yet, get them in a room together and present your report to them. Let them know that you really want to hear their reactions and feedback. You want to be absolutely certain that they agree with what you've written. If there are insights you've identified that they don't agree with, you need to know at this point. If there are functional benefits that they think are critical, you need to know which ones they are. If you disagree with them in terms of the key emotional end benefit offered by the brand, or they disagree amongst themselves, this is the forum for exploring where that disagreement comes from and to try to find a resolution.

If you don't have agreement from your stakeholders on the building blocks of your brand positioning, you probably won't have agreement on the positioning either and it's likely to fall apart at the executional level. It's far better to take the time and go to the effort of achieving consensus at this stage. People who have been involved and engaged are much more likely to be supportive in the long run. Who knows, you might even discover that you didn't have it quite right in your own mind and end up with more clarity yourself for having run it by your stakeholders.

## ORGANISING YOUR SUMMARY OF LEARNINGS REPORT

Here's an outline that you can start with to structure your report. You may find that there are specific topics that you need to cover that aren't included in this prototypical version, so feel free to adapt it to your purposes.

Remember that this is a report on learnings, not the final recommendation. Even though it contains many of the same headings as the brand positioning, you are capturing everything you learned under each of the headings at this stage. You may want to talk about different perspectives amongst stakeholders and hypothesise about why they exist, comment on changes in key factors over time, acknowledge gaps between current and ideal perceptions, etc. There will be time later for editing what you've learned into a final recommendation.

 This outline also appears in your workbook on page 37.

1. Background and Introduction
    a. Summary of how the project came about and what motivated it Project 'owner' and key deliverables
    b. Summary of the process undertaken to reach this point
        i.   Information collected
        ii.  Research conducted
        iii. Stakeholders consulted

2. Category Overview
    a. Category Definition
    b. Growth trends in the category
    c. The rate of change and innovation in the category
    d. The level of differentiation amongst key competitors
    e. The core needs that this category fulfils for its customers
    f.  The key drivers of brand choice

3. Business Overview and Objectives
    a. Business history
    b. Current state of the business
        i.   Sales
        ii.  Market share
        iii. Key competitors
        iv.  Strengths and weaknesses
        v.   Opportunities and threats
    c. Business objectives
        i.   Sales
        ii.  Market share
    d. Current brand positioning
    e. Summary of challenges and opportunities

4. Competitor Overview
    a. Market share
    b. Positioning
    c. Strengths and Weaknesses
    d. Samples of their marketing and communications materials
5. Customers and Prospects
    a. Demographic description
    b. Priorities, if multiple customer or prospect groups identified
    c. Be specific if there are prospect groups not currently engaged by the brand
6. Brand Attributes
    a. The tangible, physical elements that make up the brand and its offer

# STEP FIVE – WRITE THE BRAND POSITIONING

In this chapter you're going to get down to the task of actually drafting your brand positioning, drawing on all the preparation and thinking you've done up to this point. It's the most important step, because it's where you actually devise the flag on the hill that will drive all the decisions you and the team need to make. But having said that, don't get caught up in over-thinking the content of each box in the model.

This is your first draft and there will be plenty of opportunity to refine and sharpen it using the guidelines in the next chapter. More is better in this part of the process, to a point. I'd rather see you write two pages of target audience insights for now and worry about narrowing the list down to the key insights in a second or third draft. The same applies to attributes, functional benefits, personality, etc.

 So grab your workbook (page 39) and work through the content guidelines for each heading.

## WHO WE TARGET

### Category

 You've already done this work as part of chapter 6, so you're already well on your way. Pick up your final summary of your category from page 20 of your workbook and transfer it to page 39 to kick off the writing of your brand positioning.

### Target Audience

The target audience is the group of people you want to motivate to buy your product or service. They are the people you're going to engage in conversation about your brand.

This is one of the most important parts of the process to explore thoroughly. Remember that positioning your brand is about describing it in a way that will be most relevant and appealing to your target customer. In order to do that, you must have a clear picture of that target customer and how think, feel and behave in your category.

For purposes of this exercise, it's useful to focus on your ideal target audience. Most brands will have relevance to a range of people, but for purposes of developing your brand strategy, the clearer you are about the person you want your brand to appeal to, the more relevant and compelling you can be when you start having that conversation or telling that story.

With limited resources (and let's face it, pretty much every organisation has limited resources that need to work as hard as possible), it's best to focus on the target audience that represents your strongest opportunity.

If you go too broad you will end up not really connecting with anyone in a meaningful way.

A good way to tackle this part of the model is to imagine a single person who would represent your best prospect. Think of them as the person your brand could do the best job for. This is slightly different to picturing your preferred customer. Don't fall into the trap of writing variations on 'someone rich who loves everything about my product and buys millions of dollars worth.' Nice idea, but not useful from the perspective of writing your brand positioning.

Under this heading, we're only talking about the nuts and bolts, or demographics of the target audience. As a starting point for painting a picture of that customer, consider the following headings:

- Demographic description
  - Gender

    Is your brand purchased mainly by males or females? It's fine if it will be purchased by both, but if that's the case you'll want to be confident that the story you need to tell the women and the men is the same, or you'll need to target them separately. Focus is the key. And remember that we're making a distinction between the purchaser and the user. They are not always the same person and you need to work out which you're talking to.

  - Age

    It's useful to be fairly specific here. While it's true that lots of brands cross a wide age spectrum, it's likely that the nature of the appeal of the brand or the relationship with the brand will differ between an 18-year-old and a 40-year-old. If the age spectrum is wide, it will be useful to break it down into finite ranges for individual targeting and/or to decide on a primary target audience that is most relevant to your brand.

  - Income

    How much money does the target audience need to earn to be a genuine prospect for your brand? There's often a distinction to be made between individual income, household income and disposable income. For example, you may be targeting a young person with limited individual income, but whose household income (including their parents) is significant.

- Employment Status

  It may be relevant to specify whether the target audience is
  employed and, if so, at what level (full time, part time, casual, etc)
  in order for them to be the right prospect for your brand.

- Occupation

  In addition to whether they are working, it may be relevant to talk
  about what they do for a living. This isn't always relevant, but you
  may want to make a distinction between white collar and blue
  collar as a factor that makes someone a better prospect for your
  brand. There may occasionally be very specific criteria here,
  for example if you're selling a business-to-business product or
  equipment that is specifically relevant to a particular industry
  or job.

- Education

  Is someone with a university education more likely to be interested
  in your brand? Or do you have an offer that's designed to appeal
  to people with less education? Remember that the higher the
  level of education you specify, the narrower your target audience
  becomes. This can be a good or a bad thing, depending on what
  you have to offer.

- Ethnic or Cultural Background

  While your brand might have equal relevance to people across any
  number of ethnic or cultural groups, the way you need to position
  it and the nature of the conversation you need to have with them
  can vary tremendously, so if there are specific ethnic or cultural
  groups in your market, it's very valuable to identify them up front.

- Life Stage

  If someone's just starting out as an adult, sharing with other
  singles, living as a couple, raising a young family, providing for
  a growing family, downsizing as empty nesters, living on their
  own as a widow, or any variation in between, it may very well have
  relevance for the conversation you want to have with them and the
  way you frame up what you have to offer. Your brand may only be
  relevant to one or a couple of those stages, so you would make
  the decision to single out only the right group to talk to.

- Geography

  If your product is only available in certain geographic areas or you
  can't provide your service beyond a certain distance from where
  you're located for whatever reason, it makes sense to specify that
  your target audience includes only people in that geographic area.

> You might also want to specify that your target is people in metropolitan areas or suburban or regional areas.

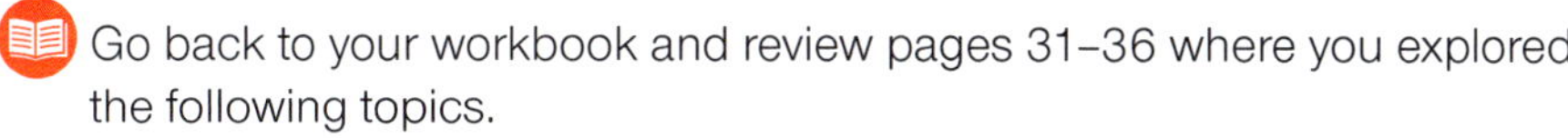 You collected information on this topic in the section of your workbook on Information and Insight Gathering (pages 29–30).

The next step is to go to page 39 of your workbook and concisely summarise a description of your target audience by editing down the information you gathered earlier.

## Target Audience Insights

As a brand, you're going to want to have a conversation with this person, so you need to paint a vivid picture of them before you can really engage them in the conversation about your brand.

Imagine you were going onto a computer dating service and were sitting down to describe the person you wanted to meet. If all you put down was age, income and hair colour, you'd probably end up with a long list of candidates from their database, but it probably wouldn't do a very good job of screening for people you would click with or have something in common with. You wouldn't have a clue what to talk about with them.

This is where we explore the relationship your target audience has with the category and the brand. There may be differences between the way the target audience thinks, feels and behaves in the category and how they think feel and behave with your brand specifically. There may be gaps between how they currently think, feel and behave versus how they ideally would if the strength of your brand were maximised. If situations like these exist, it's a good idea to acknowledge it up front. Be realistic, though, and make sure you are thinking from the target audience's perspective, not your own as the owner or manager of the brand.

Go back to your workbook and review pages 31–36 where you explored the following topics.

Q   Frequency of purchase
  –   Is the product or service something that people buy daily (like coffee), weekly (like many supermarket items), yearly (like insurance products and many memberships or subscriptions), or less often (like cars or white goods)?

Q   Purchase decision-maker and influencers
  –   Is it something they buy for themselves or for others?
     »   If they buy for someone else, who is it?
  –   Are there other people who influence their decision?
     »   An end user like the family member who requests the product

- » An expert, like a doctor or painter or chef, who recommends the product
- » A celebrity, like an actor or musician, who endorses the brand
- » A blogger, friend, neighbour or colleague who is a user of the product
- » A boss, a potential partner or local opinion leader they are they are trying to impress by buying the product

**Q** Repertoire/switching behaviour
- Is this a category where people tend to use a number of different brands, either in rotation or as part of a repertoire?
- Is brand switching frequent and casual or more considered and infrequent?
- How loyal are people to brands in this category?
- Do people have a set of brands in the category that they are happy with and choose from on any given purchase occasion, or do they tend to stick to one brand? If there's a repertoire of acceptable options, what are they? What do they have in common? What differentiates them from each other?
- Do people have different brands for different circumstances or situations, like perfumes that they choose from based on the season or restaurants that they choose from based on the occasion?
- Brand and product usage patterns
- Is this a product category that is used/consumed individually, like toothpaste, or is it more social, like beer?
- Is usage based on habit or convenience, like choosing the supermarket that's closest to home, or is it more considered, like choosing a television based on new technology and features.
- Is there seasonality to the purchase, or any other cycles and patterns?
- Is there a process that people follow in deciding what brand they buy in this category, or particular drivers and selection criteria they are likely to use?

**Q** Level of Commitment/Involvement
- Is the purchase a big commitment, like choosing a builder for your new home, or a very small commitment, like buying a chocolate bar.
- Do they like shopping/buying in this category, like wine or fashion, or do they resent it and buy only grudgingly, like insurance?

- – Is it high-involvement category for them, where they give a lot of thought to their preferred brand or brands, or is it a category where they don't feel strongly about one brand vs. another?
- – Is each purchase occasion considered and planned, habitual or more on impulse?

**Q** Barriers
- – Are there any barriers they see to considering or choosing your brand, assuming they are aware of it?

**Q** Key Drivers of brand selection and brand satisfaction
- – How important are factors like price, customer service, convenience and range in getting a customer to choose your brand over a competitor's?
- – Are there other specific factors in your category that have a major influence on what brand people choose?
- –  Once a customer has chosen a brand, what factors drive their satisfaction with that choice and keep them coming back? This could include loyalty programs, follow-up communications, service agreements, added value products, subscriptions, etc.

Then we can dig a little deeper, exploring insights into attitudes and beliefs about the category, brand and product.

**Q** Is it a category that makes them feel insecure and prompts them to look for reassurance, like used cars or high tech products?

**Q** Is there any sort of prestige or status associated with this category, like yachts, or with particular brands in the category, like Mercedes or Rolex?

**Q** Do people use the brand as a 'badge' and exhibit it openly, like a Ferrari sports car or a Louis Vuitton handbag, or is the brand invisible when it's consumed, like sugar in your tea or the internet service provider you use?

**Q** What is the target audience saying about themselves when they choose your brand relative to others in the category?

**Q** Are people comfortable with the category, like tea or breakfast cereal or is it intimidating, like advanced technology or pharmaceuticals?

**Q** How does this category make people feel in general – happy, relaxed, reassured, proud, confident, in control?

**Q** How well does your brand perform relative to others in the category?

**Q** How well known are the various brands in the category?

**Q** Is there a clear leader in the category? What is it about how consumers perceive it that makes it the leader?

**Q** Where is your brand? Is it a leader, a follower?

Q  How is your brand perceived by the target audience?

Q  Is your brand clearly understood?

Q  How do people feel about buying/using your brand relative to others in the category?

Q  What is the image of your brand relative to others – cutting edge or out of date, innovative or conservative, traditional or contemporary?

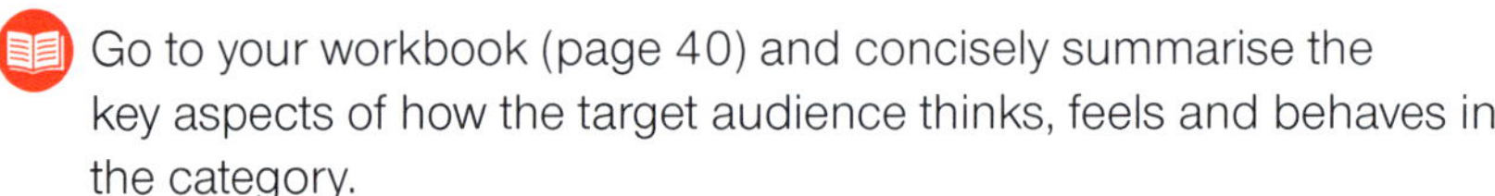 Go to your workbook (page 40) and concisely summarise the key aspects of how the target audience thinks, feels and behaves in the category.

## WHAT WE DO

Now we begin to build the brand story, using the building blocks of the Nutshell Brand Positioning Model.

### Attributes

There's a character called Joe Friday in a TV show called Dragnet that I remember from my childhood. Joe was a tough, serious detective type who solved a new mystery every week. He was famous for getting what he needed from witnesses and staying focused on 'just the facts'. His deadpan delivery of 'just the facts', became the stuff of legend and parody.

Attributes are the physical tools in the toolbox that you use to build your brand story. They facilitate what the brand does, but they are not the action or the benefit of the brand.

This heading in the Nutshell model is your opportunity to interrogate your brand and list just the facts.

This should be the easiest list to compile. It's made up of the physical, tangible, observable pieces of the puzzle, the things that aren't open to interpretation.

Here are some examples to get you started:

| BRAND | ATTRIBUTES |
| --- | --- |
| A Boutique Home Builder | Clever design; flexible floor plans; high level of inclusions and quality finishes standard; take on limited number of projects; specialise in SE suburbs; 'Plain English' operating style; staff all experienced in housing; high degree of contact between client and staff, including building supervisor; specific staff assigned and dedicated to each project – no 'call centre'; very detail-oriented; commit to commencement and completion date. |

As you can see, the attributes aren't all 'things', but they are tangible, observable elements of the story that channel up into what the brand does functionally and what it offers as an emotional end benefit.

| BRAND | ATTRIBUTES |
| --- | --- |
| A Dance Studio | **Content**:<br>Primarily dance, covering wide range of styles;<br>Secondarily singing and acting;<br>The latest trends and styles;<br>The best choreography;<br>Four 'streams'<br><br>**Staff**: International; Current industry professionals;<br><br>**Facilities**: Grand, impressive, modern, light; parent viewing area; secure, arts precinct<br><br>**Other**: Audition-based; real performance opportunities; Eisteddfod success; RTO; 23 year history |

Again, not all the attributes are 'things', but they are the building blocks of the offer of the brand. In this case, it was useful to group the attributes under a smaller number of headings, to help organise them. As you get into your list of attributes, you may also find this useful.

| BRAND | ATTRIBUTES |
| --- | --- |
| A Boutique Microbrewery | • Owned and operated by the guys who started the business 12 years ago and they've pretty much done nothing else in those 12 years.<br>• Victoria's longest-operating active microbrewery |

This example had a very concise list of attributes, which was all they needed to build up to their brand story about being obsessive about their product.

| BRAND | ATTRIBUTES |
| --- | --- |
| A therapeutic skin lotion | Comes in a variety of forms; absorbed quickly; fragrance free; dermatologically tested; ingredients like mineral oil, lanolin oil, etc |

There's nothing especially exciting in this list of attributes, but that shouldn't concern you. It's important to know that your point of difference and key promise don't have to be driven at the attribute level. The attributes of this brand supported a positioning that was about meeting the needs of a specific market niche, but they didn't define the story for the brand. Attributes are often rationale points, or reasons to believe the core promise of the brand.

 Go back to your workbook now (page 40) and list the key attributes that define your brand. Not everything that's true will be relevant in positioning your brand and telling your story, but here are some of things you might want to list for consideration:

- Where you are based
- How long the brand has existed
- The size of the business
- The ranking of the business in its category, or its market share
- Any particular machines or equipment that are key to the operation
- Credentials, defining traits or skill sets of staff and key people
- Functional areas/departments that add credibility to your offer

- Awards, degrees, awards, accreditation or other symbols of competence
- Key functional areas you cover for your customers
- Key building blocks, ingredients or components of your product(s) or service(s)
- Product forms or variants that make up your range

## Functional Benefits

The question to be answered in this section is 'what does your brand **do**?' We're still in the practical, rational realm here. In cool, unemotional terms, what is the function of the brand?

You'll probably find that answering the question 'what does your brand do' will use words like:

- provides
- gives
- achieves
- makes
- offers
- creates

Ways of asking the question to discover the functional benefit of a brand include:

Q   What function does it perform?

Q   What practical outcome does it achieve?

Q   What is its job?

Q   What does it do that helps the user?

Q   What role does it play in the life of the user?

Q   What skills or abilities does it impart to the user?

For example, a laundry detergent makes white clothes whiter. That's its functional benefit – 'makes white clothes whiter'.

As you can see, we haven't moved too far from a 'just the facts' approach yet. You want to articulate what your brand does, without emotional loading or a tone of 'selling' at this stage.

The brand uses or leverages its attributes to do something, or perhaps a variety of things. This is about choosing the most important one to leverage in telling the story of the brand. It's possible to include a few functional benefits, if they tie together at a higher level of the emotional end benefit, or the core need the brand meets. So don't worry about editing yet.

Here are a few more examples of functional benefits:

| PRODUCT | FUNCTIONAL BENEFIT |
| --- | --- |
| A children's performing arts academy | Teaches children to sing, dance and act |
| A boy's college | Encourages development of all aspects of the individual |
| An accountancy body | Helps their members maintain best-practice skills |
| A university | Tailors courses to the needs and background of the individual |
| A theme park | Provides a wide range of rides for kids and families |
| A skin cream | Moisturises dry skin |
| A mascara | Lengthens lashes |
| A personal trainer | Gets people fit |
| A diet program | Helps people lose weight |

## End Benefit

As discussed in Chapter 4, this is the 'so what factor'.

You'll remember that the sorts of questions you're answering here are:

Q  How does the target audience feel when they buy/use the brand?

Q  What's in it for the target audience to choose/use the brand?

Q  What need is the brand fulfilling for the target audience?

Q  What does the target audience ultimate get out of their engagement with the brand, psychologically or emotionally?

You might know the classic quote attributed to Charles Revson, founder of Revlon – 'In the factory we make cosmetics; in the drugstore we sell hope.'

When he started the company, he made nail polish. So, he was initially in the business of manufacturing nail polish, which is quite clear and understandable. But it's also limiting. Then he added lipsticks. Later he added perfume, etc. Interestingly, in his famous quote about selling hope, Revson leapfrogged all the rational, manufacturing-based definitions of his category definition. He went straight to an emotional, big picture definition of what business he was in. He declared that Revlon was in the business of hope. Wow!

How dramatically different is that as a basis for framing up the story you want to tell and the conversation you want to have with your target audience? Revson was very clever to make that leap, because he understood that a woman is making much more than a rational decision about what colour nail polish or lipstick she wanted. She's making a statement about herself, creating an image for herself. Cosmetics are in the business of helping make that statement.

By starting with some clarity on what the target audience is looking to get out of their relationship with the brand on an emotional or psychological level, it helps keep us on track in working through the discussion of what the brand does, functionally and emotionally.

I'd like to go into a bit more detail now around the need that the brand is responding to for the target audience. The need that the brand is fulfilling is directly linked to the end benefit the brand provides.

On the next page is a model that may help kick start your thinking on this somewhat abstract topic. It is based on the work of Carl Jung in the early part of the 20th century, which continues to be used by marketers, human resources managers, psychologists, etc. in many forms today. This version comes to me from one of the best qualitative market researchers I have ever worked with, Tracey Rankin from Alchemy Research and Insights in Melbourne.

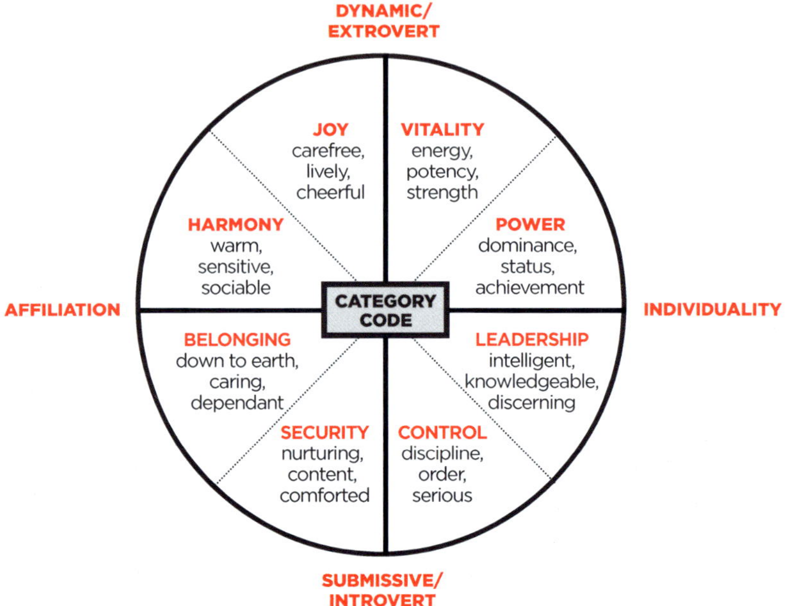


Without getting too technical, the model behind this is based on the idea that how we behave, process information, make decisions and generally interact with the world around us and can be broken down around two axes.

The vertical axis is how you relate broadly to the world – either more inwardly (protective, or introverted) or outwardly (expressive, or extroverted). The protective end is about preserving the status quo and resisting change, where the expressive end is about pushing the envelope and exploring new things.

The horizontal axis is about how you relate to others – focusing on either the group (affiliative) or the individual (independent). I think of it as 'about the group' versus 'about me'.

On a broad level, those two axes create four quadrants. Let's review them, working clockwise from the upper left hand quadrant:

- The upper left hand quadrant is expressive/extroverted and about affiliation with the group. The core need is about sharing good times with others.
- The lower left hand quadrant is also about affiliation with the group, but it is more introverted and protective. The core need is more about feeling safe and connected.

- The lower right hand quadrant is introverted and protective as well, but this is paired with individuality and standing apart from the group. The core need is to protect yourself from criticism and loss of control.
- The upper right hand quadrant is still about individuality and standing apart from the group, but it is expressive/extroverted. The core need here is about experience and achievement on your own terms.

Going further, this model uses the interaction of the two axes to create a range of eight fundamental need states, or motivations. Each has a name that is used as a starting point in laying out the model. That basic model provides a sort of landscape of human nature and the needs that drive us.

Most categories and brands respond to multiple needs, so don't think that you need to figure out the one need that is 'correct' for your brand. You will probably want to focus on one when it comes down to telling the core story of your brand, but we're not up to that point yet.

Here's an example of how a category or brand can fulfil multiple needs. Take radio as a category:

*Vitality* – Radio can liven you up, keep you energised, motivated and moving. This need fits in the upper right hand part of the model because it's 'about me' and it's very extroverted, in the sense of activity and momentum.

*Power* – In the radio category, the core notion of 'power' from the model is expressed 'status'. Like 'vitality', it is in the upper right hand quadrant and is about extroversion, but it's shifting the balance more towards the horizontal access about standing apart from the crowd. 'Your' radio station can be worn like a badge, asserting your individuality and helping you feel different from the masses and superior.

*Competency* – Listening to the radio can answer a need to feel knowledgeable, in the know and on top of things, whether it's news, traffic, or even celebrity gossip. This position in the model is about asserting yourself ('about me'), with a focus on mastery of how things are. The need for competency is about making sure others don't see you as being caught out or taken by surprise.

*Control* – Control in this case is control over your environment, where radio fills a need to block out distractions and help you focus. It's still 'about me', but with a greater emphasis on keeping things as they are, not letting external influences get the better of you.

*Security* – Now we're over on the left hand side of the model, where it's 'about the group'. In this position, the need is defined by a strong emphasis on protection. For many people, radio is a way of satisfying a desire for companionship and reassurance, to avoid feeling alone.

*Unity* – Shifting one position further around the model, it's still about protection, but with a greater emphasis on the group. That translates into knowing that there are lots of other people listening to the same radio program, which can fulfil a desire to feel part of a group or community – part of mainstream society.

*Harmony* – This is similar to Unity, which makes sense because we're in the 'about the group' part of the model and Harmony sits next to unity. The difference with Harmony is that it's a little more extroverted, so in this case radio responds to a need to feel uplifted, engaged, connected, in a light-hearted and positive way.

*Joy* – This position in the model emphasises the extroverted, outward-focused need for expression, combined with the sense of being 'about the group'. This translates into radio's ability to provide a release from stress, tedium or worry, in order to enjoy and get the most pleasure out of life.

It's easy to imagine one radio station delivering on more than one of those needs. It's also easy to imagine one person looking to fulfil several of those needs at different times, in different situations.

So, use this model as a thought-starter to explore what people in your target audience are looking for that your category and brand can provide.

Let's continue the examples presented in the section on functional benefits and build on them, to bring this to life a bit more.

| PRODUCT | FUNCTIONAL BENEFIT | END BENEFIT |
|---|---|---|
| A children's performing arts academy | Teaches children to sing, dance and act | Help children to express themselves. Give them confidence and social skills so they are happier. |
| A boy's college | Encourages development of all aspects of the individual | Give my child every opportunity. Feel like a responsible parent. |
| An accountancy body | Helps their members maintain best-practice skills | Career advancement and a feeling of confidence. |

| PRODUCT | FUNCTIONAL BENEFIT | END BENEFIT |
| --- | --- | --- |
| A university | Tailors courses to the needs and background of the individual | Opportunity. Self-belief and the ability to achieve their dreams. |
| A theme park | Provides a wide range of rides for kids and families | Fun and excitement. A shared experience of bonding for the whole family. Lasting memories. |
| A skin cream | Moisturises dry skin | Relieves self-consciousness and makes me feel more sensual and attractive. |
| A mascara | Lengthens lashes | Attracts the attention of others and puts the focus on me. Helps me stand out in a crowd. |
| A personal trainer | Gets people fit | Increased self-confidence. Regain a youthful, active lifestyle. |
| A diet program | Helps people lose weight | Rediscover a feeling of vitality, attractiveness and control. |

Remember, you're trying to identify a deep level where your brand can meet a need that's relevant to the category and important to your customer. Put yourself in your customer's shoes and think about why it's important to them to get the outcomes the brand provides at a functional level.

 Now, it's time to go to your workbook (page 42) and capture the key needs addressed by your brand.

Make sure you're layering up from the functional benefits you've identified to add a compelling end benefit to the story you're building for your brand. If you're not sure yet what the most compelling end benefit might be, capture any that you think are relevant and we'll edit later.

## Fitting the pieces together

If the model is working, you will see a linear connection from the attributes to the functional benefit to the emotional end benefit.

In rough terms, the logic is:

- 'Because the brand has' **or** 'using our' _________________ (attributes)
- 'we can do' _________________________________ (functional benefit)
- 'so that you feel/achieve' _____________________________ (end benefit)

The target audience is at the heart of this thought ('so that **you** feel/achieve…'), which reinforces the point that the whole brand positioning needs to be grounded in clarity on what audience you're targeting.

You might want to use the model to consider the category as well as your specific brand and what it offers within the category. You might end up choosing a specific need or needs from the list of needs met by the category. Or you might take what you see as the primary need for the category and identify a twist on it that is more relevant to your brand.

Lynx deodorant is a good example of the latter. The deodorant category addresses a need for confidence. Lynx combined that with the target audience of young men, and came up with a very specific need state – confidence in their attractiveness to girls. This specific need state becomes the consistent, single-minded focus of the brand.

 Complete this exercise on page 43 of your workbook.

## WHO WE ARE

## Brand Personality

### What is the personality of your brand?

This can be a difficult aspect to work through, because it feels quite abstract to some people. It's important though, because the reality is that people don't always give a lot of conscious thought to the brand they buy in a particular category. Sometimes they just buy the brand they 'like'. And that doesn't necessarily mean the one that tastes or looks best. It's often a question of the personality of the brand. Liking a brand can be the tie-breaker in a crowded category or one where it's difficult to differentiate on a rational basis.

If you were stuck on a desert island and there was only one other person there, you would probably connect with that person for practical, function reasons. You wouldn't need to know much about their personality or values to decide whether it was valuable to you to have them in your life.

But our lives today are more like a party where there are 50 new people you haven't met before or at least don't know well. In that situation, you will probably gravitate towards the one or two people you instinctively like most.

It's the same with brands. In almost any product or service category you can name, we're bombarded with choice. We buy the brands we like, and that's not always a direct result of rational elements like functionality and performance. In a world of extensive choice, liking a brand can be enough to tip the scales in its favour.

A classic way to explore brand personality is through projection techniques.

Close your eyes for a few seconds and relax. Let the idea of your brand fill your thoughts. Not the rational things about deadlines and spreadsheets and margins, but the essence of what the brand is all about.

Now allow yourself to think of any person, alive or dead, real or fictional, famous or just someone you know, who reminds you most of your brand, if your brand were a person.

Don't worry about whether you can explain it rationally. In fact, in some ways it's better if you can't explain it. You want to come up with someone who is a similar kind of person to the person your brand would be if it came alive. Let yourself think laterally.

Okay? Once you have someone in mind, just let your mind explore who that person is and what they're like. Relax and let it be informal and playful. It's a game, after all.

Now go a step further. Think about who would be the best friend of the person you've been thinking about. Who would this best friend be? What would the two of them have in common? What sort of personality traits do they share that makes them good friends?

Jot down your thoughts on all of this in your workbook (page 44). Chances are it will give you a very good summary of the ideal personality of your brand.

There are lots of variations on this sort of projection exercise. It can be lots of fun if done in a workshop setting with a group of people. You can get people to think about the brand and then think about what sort of car or dog the brand would be, if it were magically transformed into one of those things. It's also useful to continue the exercise and talk about what sort of car or dog each of the key competitors would be. The key to this exercise, though, is to explore **why** the respondents made an association between a brand and a particular breed of dog. It's the adjectives and phrases that they use to describe their choice of car or dog that reveals how they perceive the brand.

But if all that is a bit abstract and touchy-feely for you, here's another way to approach it.

We're using the core Jungian model again, but this time it's being used to capture a range of personality traits associated with the archetypal need states.

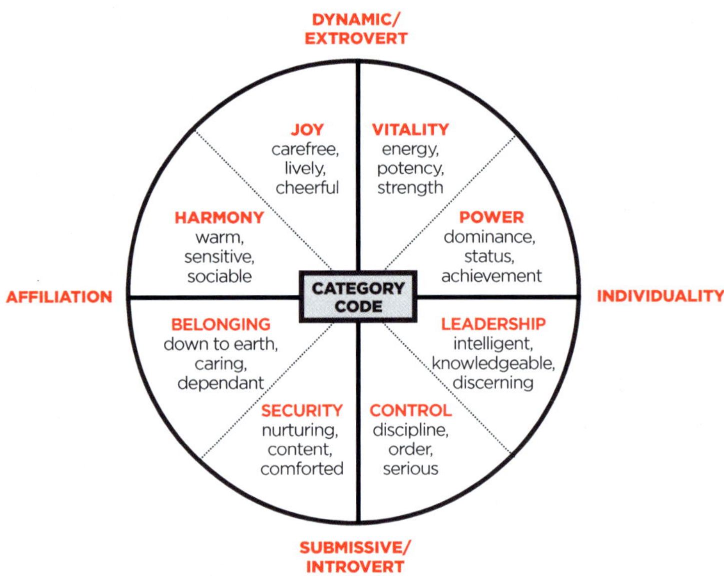


Exploring this spectrum might help you think about how you would describe the personality of your brand. If you have other words that come to mind straightaway, or feel like you have a clear image of your brand that you can capture without referring to the model, that's great. The model is just a prompt if you find you need it.

 Use your workbook once again (page 44) to write down as many personality traits as you think are relevant to the essence of your brand.

One more note on brand personality. It's easy to drift away from genuine personality words when working through this, but try to avoid that trap. Some words that people often are tempted to put in this section but actually belong elsewhere, include:

- Innovative (a trait of someone, perhaps, but not personality)
- Trusted (being trusted is an outcome related to how people react to a brand, not a personality trait). Trustworthy might come closer. Or maybe reliable.
- Intelligent – a descriptor, but not of personality. Related personality words might be intellectual, analytical, etc

Now, having developed a long list of possible brand personality words, you only need to edit it down to a concise list of key traits. Go to your workbook (page 44) for this exercise.

## Brand Values and Drivers

I described this in Chapter 4 as the 'why' factor. What are the core reasons or foundations that explain to the world why your brand makes a decision to do what it does? Ideally, what you write in this section contains an element of service – how your brand makes the world, or at least the world of your customer relative to your category, a better place.

I also mentioned in Chapter 4 that this heading is prone to clichés and motherhood statements. Part of the reason this happens is that people confuse brand drivers, which are genuinely the 'why' factor, with a list of company values, which are more about 'how' – how they aim to behave with each other and with their customers. These 'how' lists tend to be made up of words like honesty, integrity, respect, innovation and transparency. Maybe it's because I think about these things for a living and see a lot of examples of how brands are positioned, but I can't see how it's useful or compelling if everyone uses the same words under this heading as part of a brand positioning. It's a bit like the cliché of every Miss Universe finalist wanting world peace. It's certainly not differentiating.

So, you need to dig deeper for your brand. Don't make it up or say what you think will make you look good, like Miss Universe, but give some real thought to the 'why' factor for your brand.

Virgin is a brand that focuses on this part of the equation in positioning itself in the minds and hearts of its target audience. The reason it can stretch across airlines, phones, credit cards and insurance is that it stands for the principal of fighting the big greedy corporations and providing better value for money to regular people. It's a real Robin Hood type of brand. It doesn't stand for expertise in a particular field or even for any particular product. It's a brand that's based on **why** it does what it does.

This can be very lofty, as in the case of a faith-based organisation that has as its mission 'to foster human flourishing'.

More and more brands are operating from an environmental sustainability platform, where their driver is a commitment to keeping the Earth healthy for future generations, which is also pretty lofty.

But you don't have to choose brand drivers and values that will get you nominated for sainthood.

I've done work for a member-based industry body whose 'why' is a belief in the importance of their industry to the health and operational excellence of business in general.

Another example is a machine tooling company that makes parts for some of the most sophisticated jet engines in the world. Their drivers include 'relentless pursuit of perfection' and 'attention to detail'. For another company, those could be motherhood statements, but in their case they are absolutely relevant and pivotal to the fact that they get the jobs that are too difficult for anyone else to handle.

In all these examples, the common denominator is that the 'why' factor lists some fundamental truths or principles about your brand that will attract your target audience and help forge a connection and a lasting bond between them and the brand.

Look at these two examples of Brand Values and Drivers, both from universities:

**University Number One:**
- Commitment to doing what it takes to help students achieve their goals
- Offering a positive, motivating learning environment
- Responding to the changing nature of work and the workplace in Australia
- Inspiring people to learn

**University Number Two:**
- Visionary
- Global Wisdom
- Transformational
- Thought Leadership
- Social Responsibility
- Interdisciplinary

University number one genuinely describes why it does what it does, in language that relates to the markets it seeks to serve (students and employers).

University number two, at least to my ear, has described how it would like to be seen in the world, rather than why it does what it does. This list is driven by organisational ego, rather than a sense of mission or contribution.

 When you're working through the values and drivers for your brand (on pages 45–46 in your workbook), see if it helps to answer some of these questions:

Our mission is...

We believe in...

We believe that...

The fundamental need we address for our customers is...

Our greatest contribution to our customers is...

We improve our customers' lives by...

This brand is founded on the belief that...

Our core philosophy is...

If our best customers built a monument to our brand, the plaque on it would read...

The outcome that we achieve for our clients that gets us most excited is...

In everything we do, we make a commitment to...

If you're setting out to change the world, this is the place in the model to let the world know what sort of change you're trying to make. But it doesn't need to be that deep and meaningful.

Here are a couple more examples to demonstrate the range of values and drivers that can be relevant to a brand.

### A Performing Arts Academy for Young Children
- Giving students opportunities to reach their full potential
- Taking the responsibility of teaching very seriously
- Providing excellent customer service to the parent
- Creating a culture where everyone is valued

### An importer/retailer of high-end furniture

- Excellent design
- Individuality of expression
- Link between form and functionality/utility
- Outstanding craftsmanship and construction

The performing arts academy is about children and their development, so it makes sense that their end game is pretty emotional and significant. They are ultimately helping parents give their children the opportunity to grow and learn and develop into creative, well-rounded people.

The furniture retailer feels just as passionately and strongly about what they do and the contribution they make, but it doesn't sound like they're trying to change the world, because they're not. They are committed to a standard of quality that is non-negotiable and to offering a product that allows their customer to celebrate and enjoy excellence in design. The way they make their clients' worlds a better place is by offering them an opportunity for self expression that comes from owning a beautiful piece of furniture that you won't see anywhere else.

You'll need to explore this primarily with stakeholders. In talking to your stakeholders from all parts of the organisation, you're listening for things that represent the philosophies, beliefs and principles that drive the business to 'get out of bed in the morning' and do what they do. At a fundamental level, what drives the brand to do what it does?

Many people find this topic quite abstract, so you may need to listen carefully, read between the lines and prompt your respondents with your thoughts on what you think you're hearing, then ask for them to agree, disagree and discuss for further clarification.

## WHAT WE PROMISE

### Core Promise

This is the part of the Nutshell model that everything else is designed to lead up to. The intent is to take the essence of all the content of the brand positioning and capture it in a single sentence or phrase. When you've got this, you'll be able to tell someone who has never heard of your brand exactly what it's about in 10 seconds or less, as I promised in the introduction to this book.

Chances are you know roughly what the promise should be but you just struggle to find exactly the right words. You're not alone. I often say to my clients that a big part of my job is 'channelling them' to get the content right and then just finding an elegantly simple way of expressing it to achieve clarity and consensus.

More often than not it's about what to leave out more than what to put in. You want to keep it simple and focused. Often that means you end up with something that sounds obvious. Believe it or not, that's actually a good thing. You want to find the words that give you that 'Aha' moment that comes when you feel it says exactly what you want it to say and what will be most compelling to your customers.

A core promise can be, quite literally, what the brand promises:
- Committed to providing apprentice services that work for you (a registered training organisation).
- We unlock the potential of people to make significant contributions to the organisations where they work (an accountancy body)

It can also be a statement of the brand's mission:
- Ensuring that Australians get the property that's right for them (a residential property-buying resource)
- Driving positive workforce outcomes (a organisation that resolves labour disputes)

Or it can be a simple description to educate prospects:
- Connecting women with support (a social services organisation for women)
- The industry super fund that looks after the health services community (a superannuation fund specifically for people working in health services)

It can even be an invitation or call to action:
- Slow down, relax and enjoy a taste of life in the country (a regional tourism body)
- Celebrate all we have in common (a sporting event that brings together people from countries around the world)

The core promise can be quite abstract or quite tangible

- 'Imagineering' (a made-up word to evoke the combination of imagination and engineering, for an innovative technology company)
- 'Redistributing fresh, nutritious food to those who need it most' (a not-for profit that helps feed the needy)

One thing a core promise is not meant to be is a tagline. The difference between the two is that the core promise is meant to articulate clearly and rationally what the brand is trying to stand for, where a tagline is an elegant piece of writing that also needs to be memorable and consumer-friendly. Don't worry about writing poetry when you're working on your core promise. Leave that to a copywriter at a later stage.

There is really no magic formula for this last step. The art of brand positioning is to look at the model completed up to this point and to identify the most important elements from what you've written, then find a way to capture it concisely and clearly.

Remember that everything that's true about your brand won't necessarily be relevant to your target audience or go into your Core Promise. You're looking for the intersection of what the consumer wants (which you should be able to find in the target audience insights section) and what the brand does (which you will find in the attributes, functional benefits and end benefits).

You then want to capture that intersection in a way that reflects the personality and drivers of the brand.

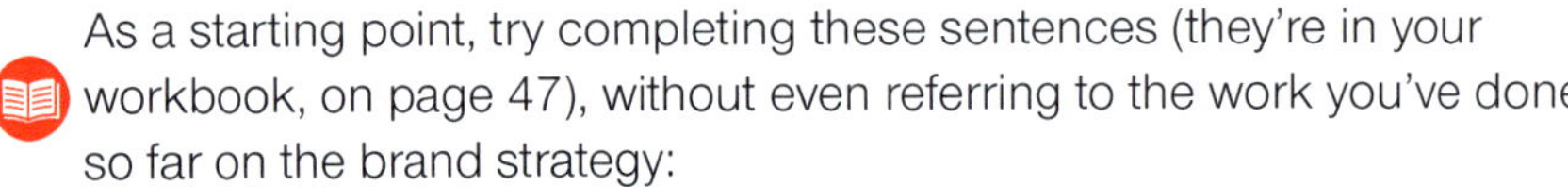

As a starting point, try completing these sentences (they're in your workbook, on page 47), without even referring to the work you've done so far on the brand strategy:

- When it comes to our customers, the promise we make is to...
- What we offer is essentially...
- What you (the customer) can expect from us is...
- The reason to choose us is ...
- The specific offer we make in our category is...
- In a nutshell, our story is...

If you find yourself writing the same thing for each of those sentences, that's okay. You're just trying to capture your top-of-mind thoughts on how to express the core promise of your brand.

Next, you might try printing out what you've written under each of the other headings in the Nutshell brand positioning model and going through it with a highlighter or a pen, marking key words and phrases that you feel are essential to telling the story of your brand to your target audience in a way that will be clear and compelling to them. Be tough. Try to highlight only the most important things. Remember that you're trying to distil this down as much as possible.

Sometimes a thought or a sentence will come together for you at this stage. But don't worry if the perfect words don't jump off the page immediately and write themselves. You might need to scribble pages of half thoughts and random combinations of key words and phrases before you start to feel like it's coming together.

Whether you highlight key words and scan them, write down sentences off the top of your head, or complete the sentence starters provided, you will almost certainly need to write down several options and leave them for an hour or even overnight, then look at them with fresh eyes and see how you react. It's a good idea to keep a note pad with you to jot down thoughts and phrases that cross your mind when you weren't even actively thinking about it. I haven't found a way to keep a note pad in the shower, but that's often when I get a flash of inspiration.

So give yourself a few days to do a brain dump, ponder, draft, ponder some more, finetune and finetune again. Sometimes when you least expect it, the right phrase will come to you and you will have your 'Aha' moment.

## Putting it together

In preparation for the next chapter, use the template in your workbook (page 49) to construct your full draft of the brand strategy. The next chapter will walk you through some stress tests to see how well it's working and tips on making it even better.

**CHAPTER 11**

# ASSESSING YOUR BRAND POSITIONING

Congratulations on completing a draft of your brand positioning. I hope you've experienced an 'Aha!' moment where you felt like what you've done genuinely captures the essence of your brand and where you want it to be.

Just before you present it to all your stakeholders and begin to march towards the flag on the hill it represents, I want to encourage you to put your draft through three tests, to see if it holds up to scrutiny.

This chapter isn't long, but it provides a mini master class to ensure that the brand positioning you've developed will guide your business to the success it's capable of.

To get started, I would suggest that you print out a copy of the Nutshell brand positioning model you completed earlier for your brand and keep it in front of you for the rest of this chapter while you're evaluating the work that you've done.

As you go through the three tests, take notes on your draft brand positioning in your workbook (pages 51–55) capturing any weaknesses or issues that arise when you're assessing what you've done so far.

## TEST ONE – CHECK THE CORE PROMISE

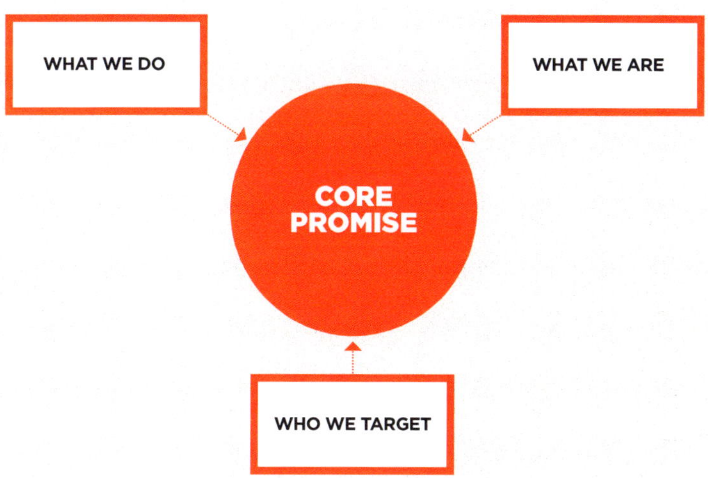


This core promise diagram represents a simplified version of the Nutshell Brand Positioning model, the upside down triangle that you completed in Chapter 10. It's a reminder that the Core Promise is meant to be a distillation of the key points in the Nutshell Brand Summary model.

Ask yourself the following questions and be disciplined in coming up with your answers:

Q   Is the promise specific and relevant to your category?

Q   Does the promise resonate with the insights you've captured about the target audience?

Q   Can the promise genuinely be delivered by the attributes and functions of the brand?

Q   Does the promise reflect the end benefit offered by the brand?

Q   Is the tone of the promise consistent with the brand personality?

Q   Are the brand drivers/values reflected in what the brand is promising?

If you can't honestly and objectively answer yes to all of the above questions, you probably need to revisit the core promise and find a way to tweak it to meet all the criteria in the list.

## TEST TWO – CHECK THE SWEET SPOT

In Chapter 3, I introduced the idea of the Positioning Trifecta and the sweet spot represented by a brand positioning that is deliverable, desired and differentiating.

Now is the time to take a critical look at the positioning you've developed for your brand and double check that it delivers on all three criteria.

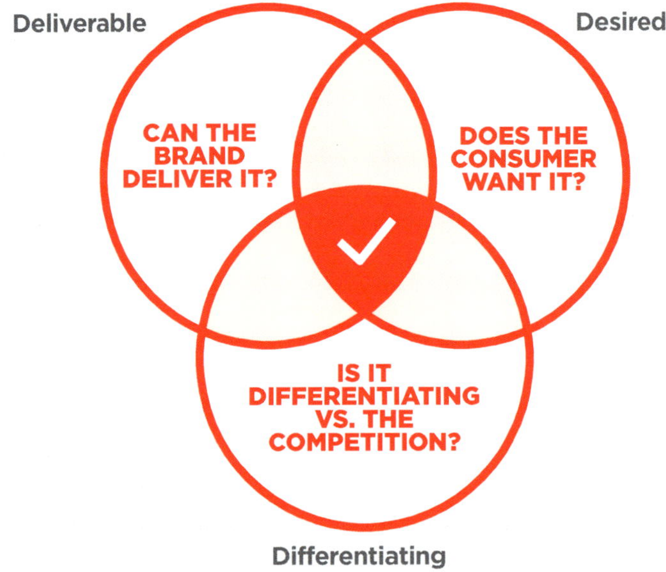

Ask yourself the following questions relative to the work you've done so far on your brand positioning:

## Deliverable

Q   Does the business have the skills, resources and capacity to live up to the core promise you're making?

Q   Were you objective in listing the attributes possessed by the business?

Q   Do the key attributes you've listed link directly to the functions performed by the business?

Q   Are there any weaknesses in the business' ability to perform the functions you've identified that need to be addressed before you can confidently deliver what you're promising?

Q   Does the end benefit flow directly from the attributes and functions you've listed?

Q   Do all your interactions with your target audience reflect the brand personality you've written?

Q   Does the business genuinely live up to the values and drivers you've listed?

## Desired

Q   Have you painted an honest, insightful picture of your target audience?

Q   Have you validated the insights about your target audience?

Q   Is the end benefit genuinely relevant and meaningful to your target audience?

Q   Will the brand personality appeal to the target audience?

Q   Will the target audience connect with the values and drivers you've listed?

Q   Is the core promise written with the target audience in mind?

Q   Is there a strong link between the target audience insights, the end benefit and the core promise?

## Differentiating

Q   Have you identified your key competitors?

Q   Have you summarised their brand positionings?

Q   Is your brand positioning different to theirs in a way that will be relevant and compelling to your target audience?

Remember that differentiation can come from:

- Attributes
- Functional benefit
- End benefit
- Personality and/or Drivers

The key is to put your brand positioning and your best assessment of competitor brand positionings side by side and ask yourself whether yours is sufficiently different in ways that will convince your target audience to choose your brand.

## TEST THREE – CHECK YOUR GOALS

The third test relates back to the circular brand management model I introduced in Chapter 3. Managing a brand is an ongoing process of assessing where you are now, envisioning where you could get to, planning how you could get there and measuring your progress towards your goals.

So ask yourself the following questions about the brand positioning you've written:

**Q** Does the category definition accommodate any growth or expansion you anticipate for the brand over the next five years?

**Q** Does the target audience represent your best opportunity for current business as well as future opportunities?

**Q** Do the insights about the target audience reveal an opportunity for you to respond to a genuine need and/or solve a genuine problem for your target audience?

**Q** Have you articulated where you want to be as a business in measurable, tangible terms?

**Q** If you deliver on the functional benefits and the end benefit in your positioning, will it lead to a change in attitudes and behaviour amongst the target audience that will result in achieving the goals you set out for your business?

**Q**  Does the core promise concisely and clearly articulate how the target audience needs to see your brand in order to take it to where you want it to be?

## SUMMARY

I know it feels like a lot to ask, but if you can answer yes to all of these questions, you can be really confident that you've developed a winning brand positioning.

If you have any doubts about what you've written, don't give up hope. Just work your way through the details of why you can't say yes to any particular question and brainstorm how you would have to finetune your brand positioning to strengthen it. You'll get there.

CHAPTER 12

# IMPLEMENTATION AND MEASUREMENT

Well done. If you've gone through the Nutshell process and worked through the headings in this book, you've got a pretty solid summary of how you want your brand to be perceived by it's target audience.

The reason the Nutshell brand summary fits on one page is so that you and everyone involved in delivering your brand to the customer can print it out, laminate it and put it on a pin board next to their desk for easy reference.

It's there as a touchstone for every decision you or anyone in the organisation needs to make about an aspect of how the brand will present itself or behave.

## TAKE INVENTORY

Start by doing a quick audit of every way the brand is manifested. It could include:

- Logo
- Tagline
- Signage
- Uniforms
- Products
- New product development
- Marketing campaigns
- PR releases
- Brochures
- Ads
- Sales materials
- Livery
- Customer service training manuals
- New staff induction manuals
- Style guides
- Sales training
- Call centre scripts
- HR policies
- Internal newsletters
- Website
- Etc.

Take the full suite of materials, products and activities that represent your brand, and put them to the test of your brand positioning. Ask yourself honestly whether each one of them is taking the brand towards the flag on the hill that you've envisaged. If anything isn't living up to your brand positioning, change it so that it does.

The brand positioning should form the DNA for every brief that you write for any supplier working with you to get your brand out there. It should be part of the checklist you use to evaluate everything you get back from them before it's approved and implemented.

Of course, there are many things your brand will do that will be tactical in nature and not intended to capture the big picture of the brand offer. For example, you may do an annual stock take sale that doesn't need to tell the core story of the brand, but it should present your sale in a way that is consistent with the brand story.

There's a big difference between the way David Jones and Kmart do sales events.

There's a reason for that. It's called the brand.

## MEASURE TO MANAGE

There's a consistent message that you will hear from very successful business people at executive levels – you can only manage what you can measure.

Think of it in terms of your business plan, where the concept tends to be more tangible. If you've set a goal of selling one million units, you've probably also set specific goals by region, by salesperson, by month, etc. You can't manage it effectively without breaking it down into these bite-sized chunks and you can't manage it at all unless you're measuring the detail of how many units you sell.

While measurable elements are often more abstract and more difficult in the case of brand positioning and marketing strategy, the principle is still vitally important.

## BRAND MANAGEMENT AS AN INVESTMENT

What's the difference between a cost and an investment? In both cases, you hand over money in exchange for a product or service. So why does a cost sound like a bad thing and an investment sound like a good thing? It has to do with what you get in return for your money.

When something is referred to as a cost, it implies that it's a drain on the business or that it generates a negative return. It's seen as something that the business has to do, with the implication that you want to spend as little money on it as possible.

When something is referred to as an investment, there's a clear implication that it grows the business and generates a positive return. It's seen as something that the business seeks to do, because every dollar the business spends doing it generates more than that dollar in return. So, naturally the business focuses on things it considers investments in the bottom line and commits its resources to those that generate the biggest return.

The reason that marketing, and especially brand marketing, is often considered a cost rather than an investment is that companies don't make the effort to measure the outcomes they produce. If they don't measure them, they can't manage them, so they end up being seen as a cost to be minimised.

I say 'especially' brand marketing, because it is the least tangible aspect of marketing. This is a classic situation that retailers deal with every day. How often do you see an ad for a store that doesn't focus on a sale or at least on specific products and prices, even if they're not on sale? Not very often.

That's because the business can measure the number of units of each product featured in the ad, multiply that by how much they make per unit and subtract the costs of making and running the ads. That gives them a tangible measure of the return on running that campaign. How do you measure the effect of running a commercial that just says 'There's no other store like David Jones' or 'Woolworths. The Fresh Food People'?

It's harder to measure and it's more abstract, but it's worth doing, because brands have value.

A detailed discussion of assigning a monetary value to brand is outside the scope of this book, but if you're interested, do a web search on brand valuation. You'll see how and why businesses assign a value to their brands that can reach millions, billions or even hundreds of billions of dollars in a few cases.

At this point in the process, you need to start focusing on marketing strategy and a marketing programme. You'll remember from earlier in the book that marketing is about getting the story of your brand out into the world.

There are plenty of other books and resources to guide and inspire you on marketing. Instead, this chapter is about the tools and disciplines that will help you to know whether your marketing is actually getting you closer to the flag on the hill.

## BRAND HEALTH

Given the value that many companies assign to their brand, both in abstract terms and as part of their balance sheet, it shouldn't be surprising to learn that there is an established framework for measuring and managing the health of a brand.

There are typically five stages, or degrees of engagement, that a person might have with a brand. They are, for the most part, linear and sequential, as depicted in the following diagram.

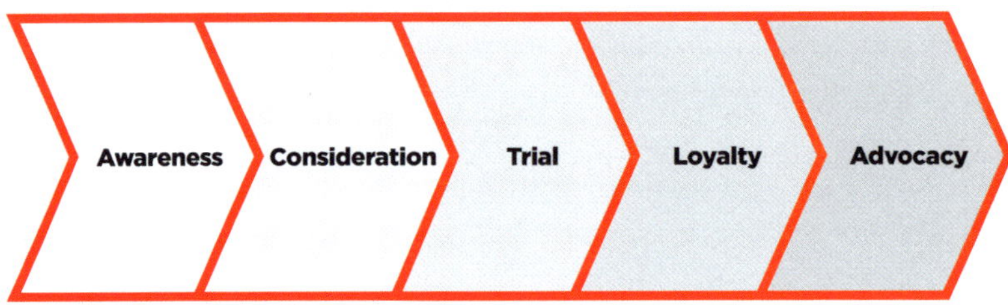


Here's an overview of the concept and the logic:
- You have to be aware of a brand before you can consider it.
- You have to consider buying it before you buy it.
- You have to try a product and decide you like it before you become loyal to it.
- If all goes well and you become loyal to a product, you may choose to recommend it to others, but you probably won't do that unless you're a fan personally.

### Awareness

Awareness is literally the beginning of the process of getting someone in your target audience to engage with your brand. Without awareness, you can't go any further.

The starting point of awareness is very basic. It's a measure of whether someone in your target audience has ever heard of your brand. It is often broken down further, however, to get a more refined measure of the strength of the awareness:

- Top-of-mind awareness
  Top-of-mind awareness is achieved when your brand is the first name that comes to mind when someone thinks of the category you're in. This is an indicator of market leadership and is what every brand aims

for. If you can achieve this, particularly in categories that are low-involvement or where purchasing is driven by habit more than active, conscious choice, you are likely to withstand attempts by competitors to win over customers from you.

In terms of measurement, the level of top-of-mind awareness you have is the percentage of people who name your brand when asked the question 'What is the first brand that comes to mind when you think of (the name of your category – soft drinks, computers, supermarkets, etc). Did you think Coke, Apple and Woolworths? If you did, those are the brands that have top-of-mind awareness in their categories for you.

- Unprompted Awareness
  Unprompted awareness includes the first brand the consumer thinks of, but also includes the full list of any others they can name off the top of their head. This set of brands is the list that the consumer will choose from naturally, without any campaigns or marketing efforts to get on their radar. If your brand has unprompted awareness with your target audience, you have a good foundation of engagement with them.

  In terms of measurement, unprompted awareness is the percentage of people who list your brand as the first one they think of in your category plus the percentage who list your brand in answer to the question 'What other brands of (your category) can you think of?'

- Prompted Awareness
  Prompted awareness, as the name implies, is when someone in your target audience recognises your brand when it's mentioned to them, but they didn't think of it without the reminder.
  Achieving prompted awareness is a good step in the right direction, but it means your brand will have to work harder to be selected, because you have to metaphorically jump up and down and wave your arms to get their attention when they're considering a purchase. They don't think of you unless you actively put your name in their head at the right time.

  In terms of measurement, prompted awareness is achieved when a consumer is shown a list and asked 'Which of the following brands have you heard of' and your brand is one of the ones they pick.

- Awareness of What? – Brand Perceptions
  Awareness is essential, but it's only the first step. It can be negative or positive. It can be vague or clear. Before you can be confident that awareness of your brand is working in your favour, you need to be clear about the specifics of that awareness – how your brand is perceived. The blueprint for the awareness you want is found in your brand positioning.

If you've completed the Nutshell brand positioning model for your brand, that one page contains all the key elements that you want your target audience to be aware of and associate with your brand. In that model, you have listed the key things that add up to the story of your brand:

- The attributes that provide the building blocks of what you do
- The functional benefits you offer
- The end benefit to the customer of choosing your brand
- The personality of your brand that will motivate the target audience to like you
- The values and drivers of the brand that will resonate with the target audience
- The core promise that summarises your position in the market.

To manage your brand effectively, you need to know whether the target audience perceives your brand the way you want them to.

Measuring how the target audience perceives your brand is a function of providing a list of words and phrases that capture the elements of your brand positioning and asking your target audience how well those words and phrases fit with their perceptions of your brand.

You can get a sense of this by simply talking to people in your target audience, but there are limitations to the robustness of this methodology. For other, more disciplined approaches, see the section on brand tracking research later in this chapter.

## Consideration

Weighing up your options and deciding on a brand to buy can take a fraction of a second. Think about when you're at the supermarket checkout, you see a display with a dozen different chocolate bars and instantly grab one because it's your favourite or because you just feel like that one at that moment.

Alternatively, consideration can last weeks or months if you're making a decision that is going to involve lots of money or a long-term commitment, like buying a car or choosing a builder to renovate your home.

Getting a measure of consideration is as simple as putting a question in a questionnaire that lists the key brands in your category and asking 'which of the following brands have you considered buying in the last week/ month/year (whatever the relevant timeframe for your tracking and the purchase cycle in your category).

In terms of managing the health of your brand using this model, tracking this particular measure shows how effective your brand positioning is at converting awareness into consideration.

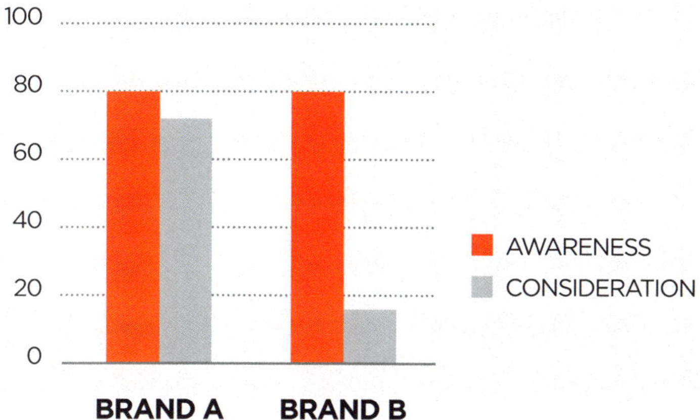


Consider this scenario. Two brands in the same category have equally high brand awareness, say 80%, which is very good. However, they have very different levels of consideration. Brand A has 80% awareness and 90% of those people say they have considered buying that brand. Brand B also has 80% awareness, but only 20% of those people say they have considered buying it.

This is bad news for Brand B, but at least if the managers of Brand B are applying the disciplines of brand health tracking, they have the tools at their disposal to work out what the problem is.

The first place to look will be in the section on measuring brand perceptions.

Does the target audience have clear perceptions of what the brand is trying to stand for? If not, it means they're aware of the brand but either don't really understand its story or don't believe it, so they are not considering the brand.

If the target audience is aware of the brand and understands its story, you might need to go back to the brand positioning trifecta and have a hard look at whether your brand has genuinely found a story that occupies the sweet spot in that model.

- The target audience might not find your brand story compelling
- They might not see it as differentiating from one of your competitors

- They might have the perception that the brand doesn't live up to its story, based on negative word of mouth, etc

If any of these problems are the cause of Brand B's poor level of consideration, brand health measures will help identify the issue and point you in the right direction to fix it.

## Trial

A person in your target audience is aware of your brand and has enough information to consider it. They like the idea of your brand based on whatever perceptions they have formed so far and they choose to get some firsthand experience with the brand by buying it for the first time. That's what trial is.

Trial tends to be relevant to brand health tracking in product categories that involve frequent or repeat purchasing, such as supermarket products or office supplies. It's also relevant to new products or services.

The notion of conversion is relevant here as well. The way we looked at conversion from awareness to consideration, we now look at the level of conversion from considering your brand to actually trying it.

Here's another scenario to consider.

Brand C and Brand D both have good awareness and good consideration levels. Let's say they both have 80% awareness and 80% of those who are aware have considered each of the two brands.

But from that point, the two brands have very different success at inspiring trial. Of those who considered Brand C, 75% tried it, but of those who considered Brand D, only 10% tried it.

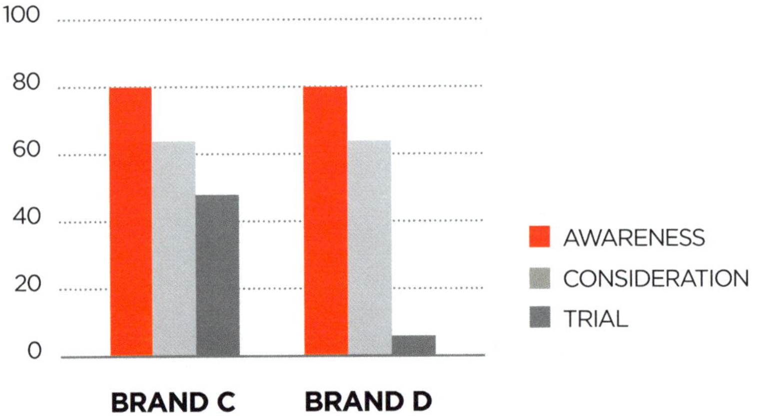

Again, the discipline of brand health measures can help understand why Brand C has moved successfully to the next stage of building a relationship with the target audience and Brand D has stalled.

It could be something operational that tripped up Brand D, like out-of stock problems, a price point that was too high, or a simple matter of convenience.  Maybe Brand C was available around the corner from the customer but they would have had to travel 15 minutes to try Brand D. If you discover those sorts of problems, it's not an issue with the story of your brand, but more a question of its ability to deliver or even make itself available.

If it is an issue with your brand positioning, it's probably an indication that you've done a reasonably good job with your brand story, but there's room for improvement:

Q   Is there a competitor that's delivering a slightly more compelling offer than yours?

Q   Have you leveraged the most important consumer insight or consumer driver of brand selection?

Q   Are you targeting a consumer niche market that's smaller than your competitors'?

Q   Is there something about the personality or values of your brand that isn't resonating with the target audience?

Q   Is your point-of-difference not as relevant or as strong as it needs to be?

The ability to compare your performance on brand health measures relative to the performance of competitors is fundamental in diagnosing the reasons for poor trial levels. For that reason, brand health research typically measures your brand as well as your competitors, allowing you to go back through the data to look for explanations about why another brand is outperforming yours on a key measure.

## Loyalty

Loyal customers are those who choose to come back to your brand time after time, rejecting other brands whenever there's an opportunity to switch.

Brand loyalty can happen at two different ends of the spectrum of brand engagement.

Some categories are very low involvement and people just buy out of habit. When they go into the supermarket, they just buy 'the one in the blue pack', often without even being able to correctly name the brand, because it's just the one they always buy. The 'brand' to them is 'the one in the blue pack', it does a good enough job at meeting their needs and it's not an important enough category to them to spend time and energy exploring options.

This scenario can work really well for the manufacturer, because they don't need to actively retain that customer and the sales just keep coming with little effort. Having said that, it's a risky scenario because the bond between the customer and the brand is weak and vulnerable to efforts from a competitor to get their attention with something new or different that stands out from the brand they've been buying out of habit.

Some categories are very high involvement and generate very strong bonds with the customer. Many people are fiercely loyal to health and beauty brands in categories like hair colour, skin creams, perfumes, etc. These products can become the person's signature and part of their identity, as in the case of a perfume or a hair colour, to the point where the person wouldn't even consider a change, for fear of losing a bit of who they are.

The Ford vs. Holden rivalry in Australia is another very good example. Many people think of themselves as a Ford person or a Holden person and adamantly defend their preference to anyone who will listen. When it comes time to replace their car, the only question for them is which Ford or which Holden will they buy next.

Loyal customers are very valuable to a business, so tracking and managing the health of your brand in order to understand what drives brand loyalty and then maximise it is an important focus of successful brands.

## Advocacy

The best thing a customer can do for your brand, aside from being a loyal purchaser, is to tell everyone they know how great it is and recommend it to anyone who is considering a purchase in the category.

If your customers are also your advocates, they become a very powerful and very credible sales force working on your behalf.

Studies show consistently that personal recommendations from people you know are the most credible endorsements when considering a brand. Even if you don't know the person doing the recommending, if you see them as a real person expressing a genuine opinion (i.e. they're not being paid to endorse the brand), their opinion can be very influential. The more convinced you are that the person making the recommendation is like you, or has similar tastes to you, the more influential their recommendation will be.

In the current age of social media, we have access to a wealth of opinions and recommendations from regular people, unpaid experts and keen amateurs. Entire business models, like Trip Advisor in the travel category, are based on leveraging the opinions of regular people. Of course, your brand has to generate positive reviews to benefit from this phenomenon.

That's why you want to cultivate brand advocacy as much as you possibly can.

## MANAGING BRAND HEALTH

You need to put a stake in the ground to commit to where you want the business to be at the end of the planning cycle.

The circular model we first looked at in Chapter 3 is relevant again here, with a more specific focus.

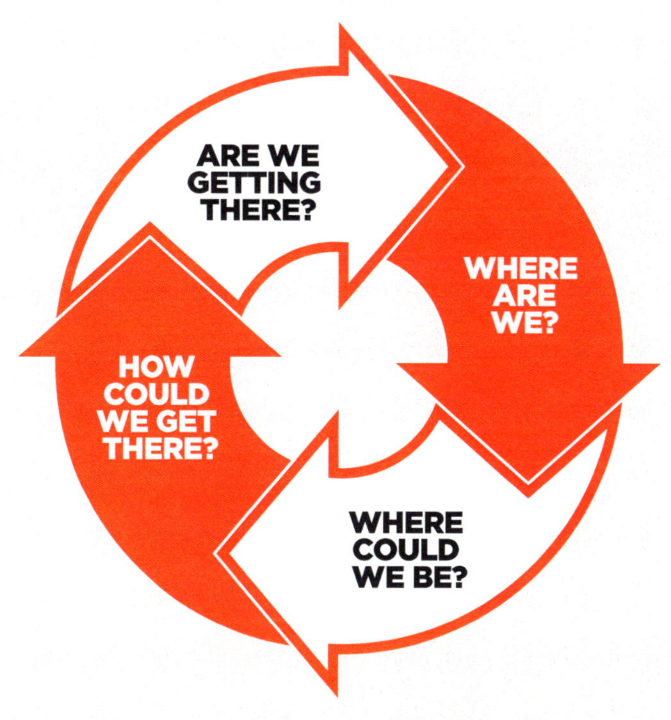

In this case, we're talking about 'where are we now' in terms of brand awareness, consideration, trial, loyalty and advocacy.

On a regular basis, it is a good idea to take a measure in the market of where your brand stands on each of these key factors.

From there, you can set objectives for where you'd like the brand to be by the end of the cycle (and in the long term). That becomes the basis for developing plans that will move the brand closer to the flag on the hill as defined by those measures. Then at the end of the planning cycle, you measure again to see whether you reached your objectives. In any case the latest measures become the new 'where are we now' and the cycle begins again. Think of it as the ongoing march towards the health and success of your brand and your business.

# CHAPTER 13

# CLOSING THOUGHTS

If the Nutshell Brand Consultancy system outlined in this book has worked for you:

- You'll never hesitate again when someone asks you to describe your business and what you do.
- You can march confidently towards success, flanked by like-minded and supportive stakeholders.
- Everyone in your organisation will make smart, strategic decisions that bring your brand to life and present it consistently and clearly to the world.
- Your target audience will understand what your brand has to offer so well and respond to it so positively that your business will go from strength to strength.

## HELP ME BE MORE HELPFUL

Let me know what has worked for you in this book and what you have found difficult, so I can improve on it in future editions.

Let me know what happens with your business as a result of working through and implementing the Nutshell model.

Visit **www.nutshell.net.au** to give me your feedback.

Wishing you great success.

Bryce Ott

CPSIA information can be obtained at www.ICGtesting.com
Printed in the USA
LVIW01n1201091017
551749LV00001B/13